THERE'S
Spaghetti
ON MY
CEILING

AND OTHER CONFESSIONS OF
A REFORMED PERFECTIONIST

ALLISON B. KELLY

ISBN: 978-1-950043-22-4

Editing and design services provided by Archangel Ink

 Archangel Ink

To my cast of characters—

Paul

Jack and Katherine

Mom and Dad

Kristin and Debbie

Thank you for being part of my story.

CONTENTS

Part IV - Sick Days and Other Ailments

Part V - Holidays

Part VI - Extracurricular Activities

Part VII - Summer Vacation

PROLOGUE

A school year has a certain linear progression. There's a beginning, a middle, and an end. And if you're an elementary school teacher like me, you might be lucky enough to have a few snow days in between. Once upon a time, I needed my life to run along a linear progression too. Back when I was a perfectionist. But life doesn't plod along in the same reliable fashion as each and every school year. Our days don't follow a set curriculum, and sometimes you learn your most important lessons when you least expect it.

I tried to give 100% to my teaching career, 100% to raising teenagers, 100% to other relationships, and 100% to myself. You don't need to be a math genius to know it's impossible to give 400% of yourself, but that's what I kept trying to do. I thought if I just could be more organized and more productive, it would all go according to plan. It didn't.

The following stories are not told in chronological order. They're not designed to be analyzed for plot development or character arcs. So, if you're the kind of person who likes to flip to the last chapter to see how it ends, there's no need. Because, really, it's the middle that's the interesting part anyway.

One September, I kicked off the school year by reading *Judy Moody* to my third graders. In this book by Megan McDonald, Mr. Todd, Judy Moody's teacher, assigns a project called a "Me collage." Mr. Todd tells the students to "draw or cut out pictures or paste things to your collage that tell the class what makes you YOU."[1] I asked my students to create their own Me collages. We enjoyed learning about each other and noticing all we had in common.

Here is a collage of stories about me, Allison, the protagonist of the story: I'm an early riser, list maker, and calendar connoisseur. I'm happy drinking black coffee, making plans, and reaching goals. I'm a teacher, a mother, a wife, a daughter, and a friend.

Maybe we have something in common.

---

1 Megan McDonald, *Judy Moody, Issue 1* (Somerville: Candlewick Press, 2000), 16.

CAST OF CHARACTERS

I am not the only person in this story. As you read, you will see a cast of characters who love and support me despite my imperfections.

Paul, my loving, extremely patient, handsome husband. He loves to sing, play guitar, and play tennis. He is always a willing participant in my adventurous plans.

Jack, my gregarious, outgoing, friendly son. He has a big smile and an even bigger heart. He is a huge Nationals fan and not a fan of his mother's nagging.

Katherine, my creative, intelligent, clever daughter. She is a party planner extraordinaire and an excellent writer. She clearly takes after her mother.

Sissa, my amazingly supportive mom. She is my biggest cheerleader and best closet organizer.

Pop Pop, my dad, who inspires me with his love of learning. He will never go "off book" because he is always reading something new.

Kristin and Debbie, my soul sisters, are the best listeners, commiserators, advice givers, and friends.

Tatum, the scene- and pork chop-stealing large, black, fluffy dog, who has stolen my heart.

Part I

All about Me

*I've always liked the time before dawn
because there's no one around to remind
me who I'm supposed to be, so it's easier to
remember who I am.*

—Unknown

IS LIFE LIKE A BOWL OF CHERRIES?

I was headed to Home Goods with my friend Katie in search of a bit of whimsy. Inspired by Jenny Lawson's ("The Bloggess") blog post about a metal chicken named Beyoncé, I decided to embark on my own quest for whimsy. My kids overheard me giggling as I read the blog and barged in: "Whaat??" I didn't let them read it because she drops the F-bomb all over the place, so I tried to paraphrase.

"Well, you see, this lady went to Home Goods to buy towels, except her husband thought she already had enough towels, so she ended up buying a really big metal chicken. She brought it home, set it up on the front porch, rang the doorbell, and hid so her husband would think the chicken did it."

Silence.

"Her husband would know it was her," Jack said.

"Wait, why didn't she get the towels?" Katherine wanted to know.

I thought it was hilarious, but apparently something got lost in translation.

I used to wish I could write like Jenny Lawson. In her memoir, she looks at some of her most challenging moments with humorous self-deprecation. Who else can write about a traumatic childhood in a way that has me giggling? She cusses and has a thing for zombies. I loved it!

In Home Goods, Katie and I perused the aisles searching for … for what? I wasn't sure. I thought I'd know it when I saw it, but nothing seemed quite right. Then I spied a wrought iron two-tiered basket. It was not at all whimsical. It was not at all what I had in mind. But it was on sale for a reasonable price and would be perfect for stocking up on apples and bananas for my family.

I've heard it said that people resemble their pets. I wonder if my Home Goods purchase reflects my inner personality. I yearn to be a whimsical metal chicken, but deep down I know I'm a sturdy, practical fruit bowl. That wrought iron basket still sits in my kitchen, holding a variety of fruits and the occasional vegetable.

That's a metaphor for my life if I've ever heard one: Some days are just peachy and other days are the pits. And you know what? I'm okay with that. You can't make fruit salad with a metal chicken.

IDEAL SELF VERSUS REAL SELF

Sissa says people generally have two versions of them-
selves: their ideal selves and their real selves. It's an
important distinction when it comes to cleaning out stuff.
Take my cheeseboard, for example.

No, really, take it. I don't want it anymore.

Because Ideal Self is quite the hostess. She entertains
effortlessly and always has a wheel of Brie in the fridge for
an impromptu happy hour. She even has a little cheese knife
with a mouse-shaped handle. Adorable! However, Real Self
has never once used this appetizer platter. Not that I don't
like cheese—I love cheese. It's the entertaining that's intim-
idating. Real Self would rather order pizza than fashion a
cheese platter. Real Self is usually in her pajamas watching
Netflix on Friday night.

Getting better at realizing the difference between Ideal Self
and Real Self makes it easier to part with things that don't
align with my lifestyle. Last year I hosted a white elephant
gift exchange. Traditionally, every guest brings an unwanted

item, but I had enough stuff to supply all the gifts myself. Admittedly, many of these were teacher gifts. Sorry, but I already have a lifetime supply of scented candles.

You know that Mariah Carey song "All I Want for Christmas Is You"? It's the one about not caring what's underneath the tree. I find myself humming this song when I think about gift giving.

Here's where Ideal Self and Real Self agree. Neither of us wants a lot of stuff for Christmas. We don't need the perfectly wrapped presents under the tree or a gourmet cheese platter. We both want to spend quality time with our family and our friends. All we want for Christmas is YOU.

I recognize that this makes it a challenge for people to shop for me. Paul has jokingly lamented that other husbands have it easy buying their wives jewelry, while I prefer a handmade coupon book of adventures. Real Self would much rather spend time WITH you than get a sweater FROM you. I struggle with gift giving too. While Ideal Self is a fantastic gift giver and wraps presents like Martha Stewart, Real Self hates shopping and usually relies on recycled gift bags.

Once Paul gave me a banjo for Christmas. I took lessons for about a year, hoping to live out the lyrics to one of my favorite songs, "Wagon Wheel." Alas, Real Self discovered playing the banjo is really hard.

With apologies to Old Crow Medicine Show, now I sing along with my altered but more accurate lyrics, "My baby plays a guitar, I dust my banjo now."

ACCOUNT DISABLED

"Your account has been disabled." This is the message I got once when I tried to log on to my blog during my vacation. Reading through the email, I saw something about security, blah, blah, and terms of service, yada, yada.

I was stunned. I had only been a "blogger" for three weeks and they cut me off! I hadn't made my mark yet! I was still finding my voice! I had all of three followers, one of whom was my mother.

After the initial shock wore off, I got angry. I tried to put it out of my mind, but I felt helplessness, frustration, and irritation seeping into everything I did. *I don't deserve this*, I thought.

Soon my anger turned to questioning. I was indignant. *WHY did they do this to me? I am a rule follower!* I actually sat and read the Terms of Service. The whole document. On my vacation. Okay, really, I skimmed it. But nothing jumped out. I racked my brain for anything in my content that could be offensive.

Oh no! My last blog topic was about doing more pushups so I could have sculpted arms like the First Lady. I wrote, "Michelle Obama, watch out!" *That's it! I've been red-flagged as a potential terrorist!* Sitting at the beach, I thought of the CIA swarming my house, wiretapping everything, and taking pictures. I knew I should have made all the beds before we left for vacation.

I returned to my account and filled out a short online questionnaire summarizing the issue. Nowhere on the form did it indicate "Check this box if you are NOT a threat to our nation's security." Soon, the response came in. Apparently, when I'd used my father-in-law's computer, Google was worried about my own security being breached. I just needed to reset my password. *Whew!* Crisis averted.

How do you handle life's little challenges? I panic first, think later, and stress and stew in between. I wish I could learn how to pause … and think first. I'd like to handle life's inconveniences with a grin, some grit, and a bit of grace. This time, it was more like a grimace, some gaffes, and a bit of grumbling. Well, at least I persevered.

I'm sure I'll have a new "opportunity" to practice soon. I'll let you know how it goes.

THE PERFECT DAY

I have a vision of the perfect day. Cloudless sky. Perfect temperature. The morning starts with a family bike ride. There's no bickering, and everyone's bike has air in the tires. In the afternoon, I sit outside on the patio with a good book. Later, friends come over to our perfectly clean house for a delicious dinner that magically materializes while I'm reading on the patio. After dinner, we sing songs and roast marshmallows by the firepit while our well-behaved dog rests nearby.

A LONGER CHAPTER

The old me never would have gotten away with the previous chapter. She would have clung to some sort of preconceived notion about how long a chapter should be.

I take that back. Because I don't think there really was an old me and a new me. I think I'm just becoming more comfortable with the real me.

I can be quite the perfectionist. When unchecked, my brain goes into overdrive to figure out how to improve. How can I use my time more efficiently? How can I be thinner? How can I be more confident, more patient, and more flexible? I think if I just had the perfect plan, I could accomplish X, Y, and Z and be satisfied.

You see, I love lists. I used to think if I got to the bottom of The List, I would be happy. Not only did I never get to the bottom of that list, The List was making me unhappy. Because I always fell short. And then I always felt like a failure. My husband, Paul, jokes that I'm like the Marines—I get more done before 9:00 a.m. than most people do all day. While it's true that I'm a productive early bird, what you don't see is the feeling of apprehension that creeps in when I've created a completely unrealistic list of twenty-five tasks I can't possibly accomplish. Instead of feeling content with the ten things I've crossed off my list, I obsess over the unfinished fifteen.

Focusing too much on my list prevented me from being present. Because my mind was always on what I was supposed to be doing next. Sometimes I woke up thinking of The List and felt sick. After a fun weekend, I would awaken Monday morning thinking of all the things I meant to do over the weekend but didn't … the chores that help me feel organized, focused, and in control for the week. It made me feel anxious. Like sweaty palms, pounding heart, pit-in-the-stomach anxious. The kind of anxious you can't explain to people because it doesn't make any sense. Like, hi, I'm in a really bad mood because I spent all weekend doing fun and meaningful things with friends and family and I didn't do enough chores.

I didn't set out to cure myself of being a perfectionist. I set out to be happier. Along the way, I realized I was happier when I was more comfortable with the real me—who I am and who I'm not. I had to accept that my house will never, ever be completely clean, straight, and organized, and I regularly remind myself that the happy chaos of life is better than a list with checked-off boxes.

As I write this, there's a piece of dried spaghetti on my kitchen ceiling. Once while cooking dinner, Paul said to Jack,

"Throw the pasta against the wall—if it sticks, it's done." Jack carefully reached into the steaming pot with the tongs and pulled out a single noodle. He cradled it in his palm and then tossed it straight up in the air. *Splat.* It landed on the ceiling and clung there like an octopus tentacle. That noodle is still stuck up there.

Taking it down is not even on my list of things to do.

Part II

Teachable Moments

You have to decide what kind of difference you want to make.

—Jane Goodall

SEPTEMBER VERSUS ALLISON

My principal says the month of September is the teacher's equivalent to giving birth: time passes, and we forget how hard labor really is. Often I say goodbye to August with high hopes and good intentions of kicking the school year off right ... then the first month of school kicks my butt instead.

September is unpacking boxes, stapling up bulletin boards, and alphabetizing class lists. September is giving a million pre-assessments, which means GRADING a million pre-assessments and then sitting in a million meetings to ANALYZE the pre-assessments. September is meeting and greeting parents at Open House and preparing Back to School night presentations. September is setting up classrooms, setting up routines, setting up conferences. September is coming to school early every single day and staying late every single evening.

And when I leave, I go to my other full-time job.

I walk in the door completely exhausted, after having been on the go for twelve straight hours, and there's laundry to be done and bills to pay. Tatum needs attention, which he demonstrates by ripping holes in my couch. There's football practice, football games, homework help, and piano practice. Everyone in my family is trying to get used to new routines and the homework load, and I am not there nearly enough for their liking. In one week of September, I was out every single night at three different Back to School nights, a driver's ed meeting, and a Girl Scout meeting. It is too much. TOO MUCH! But we all just keep going because we have to. We just keep putting one foot in front of the other and crossing off those September days, one by one.

As my students left one afternoon, I looked around the room at the aftermath of our busy day. I wanted to leave, but I had haphazardly stacked Me collages to collect, a difficult email to write to a parent, and lesson plans to prepare for the next day.

Ding!

I lifted my phone to read the text message: "Mom, I need a ride home from football."

I left my room with my to-do list looming. I picked up Jack, stopped off at home, and changed into running clothes. (Technically, it was an old hot-pink tennis skirt because all my running shorts were dirty.) Katherine picked this point in the evening to declare that she was FAILING French, so I spent a little time conjugating verbs before heading back to school at 7:00 p.m. to finish my lesson plans.

The first thing I noticed when I returned to the classroom

was that the Me collages were gone. You know, the ones I'd left in a messy pile on the floor. Mr. Jim, our custodian, thought they were trash and helpfully put them in the dumpster. Did I mention that it was raining?

Right there, standing in my classroom in my hot-pink tennis skirt at 7:00 p.m., I started to cry. I cried because the kids had worked so hard on those projects. I cried because I was trying to do TOO MUCH and I was failing miserably. I cried because it was raining. I cried because I couldn't even find the time to go for a run.

Then I heard footsteps. Coming up the ramp was Mr. Jim with a parent looking for some forgotten homework. And it happened to be the same parent that just received that difficult email an hour ago. What are the odds? So, right there, on Wednesday night, wearing a tennis skirt and holding a snotty tissue, I had a parent-teacher conference. Oh, the joy.

This story has a happy ending. The next morning when I returned to school, Mr. Jim had found the collages and returned them unharmed to my classroom.

Plus … September doesn't last forever.

October is going to rock. I am SO going to have my $#!+ together.

OCTOBER—BE VERY AFRAID

You should always be extra kind to every teacher you know all the time ... but especially in October. The end of October brings something even scarier than Halloween. It's the dreaded END OF FIRST QUARTER.

We are afraid—very afraid.

Instead of carving pumpkins, we're carving out time to add twenty-five report cards to our list of things to do. Those aren't trick-or-treaters knocking at our door—those are parents asking for a conference. Instead of making costumes, we're busy creating and entering first quarter data for our school ghouls, oops, I mean goals.

Teachers often set their sights on surviving September, thinking they'll be able to catch their breath next month. Then October hits and we realize—ha, we were fooling ourselves—this month is just as busy. New teachers often feel this phase of disillusionment the hardest. They don't have the perspective of the whole year to help them remember, *This too shall pass.*

Teachers, if you are feeling disillusioned, don't despair. You are not alone. Here are some tricks that have helped me ease the pain:

- Focus on what you ARE getting done. Self-talk is very persuasive. If you tell yourself, "I'm overwhelmed and I don't have enough time," you will feel overwhelmed. Instead, try saying to yourself, "I am having a productive day and am making progress."
- When you talk with your fellow teachers, don't spiral down the black hole of complaining— support each other instead.
- Plan small breaks for yourself. Listen to your favorite song, go for a walk, just step outside your classroom and take a few deep breaths. It's okay to skip dinner prep sometimes and order a pizza.
- Don't try to do it all. Let your family know that this is crunch time. We give tax accountants a break in April, right? Teachers need a little TLC at this time of year. Paul knows that he's on carpool duty this week. He is also a very excellent PB&J maker. You can tell he is the experienced spouse of a teacher!

Most of all, hang in there. Thanksgiving break will come. I promise.

BARF AND POOP AND OTHER COOL STUFF

"So, you actually have owl poop?" Katie asked.

"Owl pellets," Anne corrected. "It comes out of the owl's mouth. Kinda like a cat's hairball."

"Well, how often do the owls have these pellets?" Donna wanted to know.

We wanted to know more about owl pellets. Like, do they have their morning coffee and then—*Bam!*—owl pellet? It was Friday afternoon and we were planning science lessons with Anne. Anne is the amazingly wonderful, incredibly talented, knowledgeable science specialist at our school. Her job is to help the classroom teachers with their science curriculum. Next month we'll be studying food chains, animal adaptations, and predator-prey relationships. That's where the owl pellet comes in. Owl=predator. Pellet=prey.

You see, an owl swallows its prey—most often a rodent— whole. Then some cool chemistry science stuff happens in the owl's stomach and all the useful parts of the owl's meal are digested, leaving only the bones and hair of the rodent. The owl ejects the unwanted parts out of its mouth.

Anne laid an owl pellet on the table. It was about the size of an egg. She showed us how to carefully pull it apart with tweezers and separate out the bones of the rodent. *There's the skull! There's the thigh bone! Here are some rodent ribs!* They looked like tiny fish bones. She had a template of a rodent skeleton so when we found a bone, we could match it up and add it to the picture. Remember the old game Operation where you had to remove the bones from the patient? This was the reverse. We found all the bones and put them back.

We were intrigued. We wanted to know more!

"How often does this happen?"

"Several times a day," Anne said.

"Do owls also go to the bathroom?"

"Yes."

"Have you ever seen an owl eject a pellet?"

"No."

"I bet we can find it on YouTube," Jenn said.

And so, a moment later we gathered around her laptop to watch a baby owl. Even though we were expecting it, we still all screamed when the pellet was ejected. We were so loud, in fact, that some other teachers rushed into the room to see what was happening. They found us doubled over in tears of laughter.

Anne has a way of getting teachers excited about science. Anne loves science. We love Anne. Now we love science too. And owl pellets. Search the internet for "baby owl ejects pellet" and check it out for yourself. You will not be disappointed.

THE PORK CHOP STORY

"It was an ordinary Thursday afternoon when I walked into the kitchen to make dinner," I said. It was time for writing workshop, and my students were clustered around me on the carpet as I sat, pen in hand, next to a pad of chart paper.

I model the writing process by sharing stories of my life with my students. Throughout the year, they might learn about the squirrels eating Mr. Kelly's tomatoes or the rainy Girl Scout camping trip, but their favorite stories are about our crazy misbehaving dog, Tatum.

"I open the refrigerator door and start pulling out ingredients—pork chops, potatoes, and green beans. This is one of Mr. Kelly's favorite meals. Do you have a favorite meal? Turn and talk to your shoulder partner."

When I tell stories, I try to choose small moments from my life to write about. Third graders sometimes think personal narratives need to be the biggest, most exciting moment of their lives, which, at the age of eight, often involves a roller coaster ride. Their stories go something like this:

31

Today was the best day of my life. We got up and ate breakfast. Then we got in the car and drove to Kings Dominion. I got ice cream. We rode on a roller coaster. It was so fun!!!!!!!! Then we drove home and I went to bed. It was the best day ever!!!!!!

Third graders love exclamation points.

"My pork chops were simmering in my big cast iron skillet, and I was mashing the steaming potatoes when the phone rang. *Brrrinng!* It was Mr. Kelly and he sounded grumpy. 'Traffic is a nightmare and I'm going to be late. Go ahead and eat without me.'"

Depending on the focus of my lesson, I'll stop and ask students to notice different strategies. Where did I include detail and description? Dialogue? Onomatopoeia?

"Poor Mr. Kelly. 'Don't worry, honey. We will save some for you,' I told him. I filled his dinner plate with the pork chops, mashed potatoes, and green beans, covered it with tin foil, and placed it in the oven to keep it warm. Finally, I saw the headlight beams of Mr. Kelly's car pulling into the driveway. Quickly, I pulled the plate from the oven and set it on Mr. Kelly's placemat, along with a fork and a napkin. *Hmmmm*, I thought. *Mr. Kelly might be thirsty.* So I decided to run downstairs to the basement where we keep extra sodas in the refrigerator."

This is true. There are extra sodas in our downstairs refrigerator. That's not the type of beverage I was getting for Mr. Kelly after his frustrating, long day, but I don't choose to share *every* detail with the students.

"I returned to the kitchen, where Mr. Kelly's dinner was waiting. Was I imagining things? The fork was still there. The napkin was still there. The plate was still there. But the pork chops … were missing! I looked around the kitchen. Where could they have gone? Then I looked *under* the table. Who do you think I saw?"

"Tatum!" my students yelled in unison.

"That's right—Tatum. He scarfed down a feast that night. And poor Mr. Kelly ate a peanut butter and jelly sandwich for dinner."

When the laughter died down, I finished the lesson. "So, third graders, good writing doesn't always have to be about big important moments in your life. Sometimes small moments make great stories."

JOY TO THE WORLD

Do you have fond memories of a special teacher? For me, it was my second grade teacher, Miss Littman. Miss Littman, who encouraged my love of reading and introduced me to the worlds of authors like Beverly Cleary, Carolyn Haywood, and Scott Corbett. Miss Littman, who encouraged my love of creative projects, stories, and poems. When I dressed as a witch for Halloween, Miss Littman colored one of my teeth black with a grease pencil to complete the effect. When I decided to wear my favorite Ronald McDonald dress on picture day, Miss Littman said I looked just perfect.

Once, around Christmas, Miss Littman told us her favorite carol was "Joy to the World" because her name was in the song. I went home and listened to the song over and over again, straining my ears for the lyric that included "Miss Littman." The next day I came in exasperated. She laughed and told me her name was Joy Littman. I even remember Miss Littman's dog Meesha, a Husky who came to visit the classroom occasionally.

Miss Littman married and had two children of her own. We lost touch eventually. Occasionally, I try to track her down. I sure would love to tell her that she made a difference in my life. In fact, she is one of the reasons I decided to become a teacher myself.

Just what did this amazing teacher teach that I remember over forty years later? I'm sure she must have taught me how to add and spell, but I honestly don't remember much about the curriculum. I remember Joy Littman as a woman who brought creativity and a love of learning to the classroom. I remember her as human—funny and tough at the same time. She expected nothing but the best from everyone. I remember how she encouraged strengths (such as my reading and writing) and forgave mistakes (once I left school during recess and walked home!).

When I ask people about their favorite teacher, they rarely mention the curriculum. They talk about the character they developed. They fondly recall a teacher who accepted mistakes as a natural part of becoming a problem solver and a risk taker. They remember a teacher who inspired them to develop skills as critical thinkers and innovators. They remember the creative ways she made the curriculum relevant to her students' lives. They remember feeling a sense of belonging in the classroom.

As a teacher, I love December. By this time, I've had a chance to get to know my students. We've built a classroom community, so I know who is excited for the weekend basketball game and who has a loose tooth. And they've heard stories about my family—about the time Tatum ate Paul's pork chop or the time the squirrels ate all of our tomatoes. Yes, I teach them how to multiply and how to spell. I hope they will remember so much more than that.

SANTA'S PERFECT PRESENT

One year I was teaching a large kindergarten class, and I was logging a lot of hours to make it work. As challenging as teaching can be, sometimes it was easier to manage twenty-eight kindergarteners than to figure out how to parent my own two children. Coming home exhausted, I moved on to homework help, cooking, and carpooling. Sometimes it went smoothly ... but not very often.

As fall progressed into the holiday season, I was hard-pressed to find my Christmas cheer. Already stretched to capacity, I now faced gift lists, decorations, and entertaining. Around this time, my daughter asked me to mail her letter to Santa. Curious about her Christmas wish, I decided to sneak a peek before sealing the envelope.

Dear Santa Claus,
All I really want for Christmas is for Mommy to
be happy.
Love, Katherine

It was as if St. Nick himself had kicked me in the stomach with his soot-covered boot. For the first time, I really considered how my frustration and stress were affecting the rest of my family. Clearly, I was trying to do too much. What could I cut out? I loved teaching and volunteering. I loved my family, my friends, and my hobbies. I loved all the parts of my life.

Jack Welch, the former CEO of General Electric, once said, "There's no such thing as work-life balance. There are work-life choices. You make them, and they have consequences." I was trying to do a little of everything, but in seeking balance I wasn't doing any part of my life well. If something didn't go according to plan, I could feel my carefully crafted schedule crumbling, and I slipped and flailed my arms seeking anything to grab on to.

Katherine's letter to Santa made me realize that my flailing arms were bruising those around me. I couldn't be the perfect teacher and the perfect wife and the perfect mother. After reading her Christmas wish, I resolved to change. Ultimately, I realized that I didn't want to work in a classroom without being the best teacher I could be. And at this stage of our lives, the amount of time I was investing to make that happen was having a negative impact on my family. As the old saying goes, "If Momma ain't happy, nobody's happy."

Paul and I took a hard look at our finances, and I decided to reduce my hours to part-time for the next school year.

At first, I tried to justify my choice not to return full-time in the fall by filling the extra time with tasks. I made lists of ideas such as these:

- train Tatum
- improve my posture
- take banjo lessons
- clean out all the closets
- cook amazing, well-balanced meals for my family

Luckily, I realized working part-time is not about making big changes. I would still be a Girl Scout leader, Sunday school teacher, and running coach. I would still be the chauffeur, cook, accountant, and house manager. I would still clean up and mess up and dream of a well-behaved dog. And I am always going to be a wife, mother, daughter, granddaughter, teacher, and friend. I'll always love to read a great novel, ride my bike, and listen to Paul play the guitar. Changing my salary does not change who I am and what my goals are. Overall, the choice to work part-time for the year turned out to be a gift for myself and for my family. I think Santa might have had a hand in it all.

MY NO GOOD, VERY BAD DAY

I was having one of those weeks. You know, the kind where you just want to crawl out of your bed and catch the next flight to Australia?

That's where Alexander wants to move when he's having a bad day. Have you ever read *Alexander and the Terrible, Horrible, No Good, Very Bad Day* by Judith Viorst? It's one of my favorite books. One of my good friends was trying to vacation in Australia with her family one summer. However, her kids were convinced that a high percentage of poisonous animals live there, making the country entirely too dangerous. So, maybe they have bad days in Australia too. Really, I would never, ever fly to Australia if I were having a bad day because that flight has got to be about a million hours long, and I don't think I have enough Xanax to survive. I should just set my sights on the Bahamas.

Anyway, I was not lounging on the warm beach. I was right smack in the middle of winter with highs—highs!—in the low twenties. Paul was gone on a business trip, so instead of curling up in my PJs and eating ice cream straight from the carton, I had carpool duty. Then I got a haircut, and my bangs ended up too short. At school, there were just six play rehearsals left before the big class production and I kept telling the third graders, "It will all come together. It will all come together." Now I needed to talk myself into believing that. Meanwhile, I lugged a heavy bag of work home. Blech.

It's easy to get caught in a downward spiral when you are feeling overwhelmed and underappreciated. On the bulletin board above my desk, I have a yellow sticky note that reads, "Contentment is a shift in attitude, not a change in circumstance." I had to pull myself out of my puddle of self-wallowing pity to remind myself of all the wonderful things.

Like celebrating Pop Pop's seventieth birthday. Katherine wanted to make the most elaborate cake recipe ever, and we pulled it off.

We got our first snow of the year and, with it, a school delay and a chance to sleep in.

Paul returned safely from Chicago. We all snuggled on the couch together Friday night watching a family movie and there was almost no bickering.

Pausing to reflect on the good things can improve your mood. And it's cheaper than a flight to Australia.

JUST BREATH(E)

It's Saturday morning and I am nine years old. I look around my bedroom and feel unsettled by the chaos. Inside-out sweaters are slung over a chair, dirty dishes are stacked on the bedside table, and Barbie paraphernalia carpets the floor. I decide I'm going to clean my room today. Not only will I straighten up, maybe I will dust, vacuum, and organize my dolls—this could be a fun all-day project!

Excited about my plan, I head down to the kitchen to fuel up with breakfast. As I pour Frosted Mini-Wheats into my bowl, Mom looks up from the newspaper and says, "Your room is a real disaster area. I'd like you to clean that up before you do anything else today."

Phhhhht. That's the sound of my brilliant idea deflating. Suddenly the last thing I want to do is clean my room. Even though my mom is right. And I agree with her. Somehow, when she TELLS me to do it, I lose my motivation.

Fast-forward forty years to a particularly crazy week. The kind of week when you have some sort of meeting before and after school every single day. The kind of week that makes you feel like you're stuck in a Dilbert cartoon—we'd scheduled a pre-meeting before the meeting and a training to get trained for the training (aptly named a turnaround training), and my head was spinning. The kind of week where you finish one thing and move right on to the next. Gotta get it all done. No time to breathe.

On weeks like that, I feel even more anxious when I look at the calendar and see all the unchecked boxes staring at me. I know I will feel better when I make the time to slow down, get organized, and prioritize. I was trying to remind myself of that fact when I got a text from a friend.

"Just breath."

Just like that, I was a petulant nine-year-old child all over again. Instead of acknowledging that I needed to take time to slow down and take some deep breaths, I texted back, "I think you mean BREATHE."

You try to help me, I point out your typo. I can be a real numbskull sometimes.

However, I had to admit she was right. Anne Lamott once said, "Almost everything will work again if you unplug it for a few minutes, including you."[2] So I left my list of chores

---

2 Quotefancy.com, accessed October 13, 2020, https://quotefancy. com/quote/975243/Anne-Lamott-Almost-everything-will-work-again- if-you-unplug-it-for-a-few-minutes.

on the kitchen table and told my family I was feeling a little overwhelmed. I packed some workout clothes and planned to exercise with friends after school.

It was time to breathe.

THE SHOW MUST GO ON

The email arrived late Wednesday night.

I wanted to let you know that our son has been throwing up since this evening. I am not sure what is going on, but if he doesn't feel better tomorrow he will have to stay home. I know they have their big play tomorrow. I am so sorry, but I hope you understand. It is going to be a long night for us.

Poor guy. It was bad enough that he'd come down with a stomach bug—even worse to have to miss our class play. Luckily, he didn't have a singing part. Surely I could find a volunteer to read his lines for him.

Thursday morning's email brought more bad news. Another sick student. Then another. By 9:00 a.m. I was starting to sweat, and I was pretty sure my deodorant had stopped working. A violent stomach virus was sweeping through my classroom on the day of the play. We had six students absent.

Normally, I greeted my students at the door with a handshake and a smile. Thursday, I greeted them with a tub of Clorox wipes. "Desks and chairs, desks and chairs," I repeated. "Wipe down everything—door handles, surfaces, pencils, keyboards."

I explained the situation to the students. Hands shot up around the room.

"I could say the Naturalist's lines because I'm already on the stage."

"I could be the Ox and then run and change."

My students amazed me. We'd had very little time to practice due to all our snow days. We had literally lost half our rehearsal time due to closures and delays. In two short weeks, they had learned lines, cues, songs, and instrument parts. Now they were willing to do whatever it took not to disappoint their waiting audience. The volunteers refused to go onstage with a script. They quickly memorized new material and headed out for costume changes.

The lights went down. The play began. And it was wonderful! If you'd been there, you never would have guessed there were six cast members absent. Congratulations to my amazing third grade class. You pulled together and said, "The show must go on." And so it did.

CH-CH-CHANGES

After two years' worth of work, I received my endorsement in gifted education just in time to leave gifted education. Wait, what? Why would I want to leave the gifted program when I was officially certified to teach in it? Why would I want to leave a curriculum I knew and a team I loved?

I remember one particular Back to School night as a parent. I was sitting in a junior high classroom trying to listen as the teacher shared how he used guided notes in class. "Every unit I give them a new packet," he explained. "The kids read the text and then fill in the key ideas. It's basically like a fill-in-the-blank." My attention wandered to the back of the room, where the desks were turned on their sides and piled up across the tile in a line. Curiosity got the better of me, so I raised my hand.

"What are all those desks for?" I asked.

"Oh, that's from my honors section," the teacher replied. "It's a simulation activity building World War I trenches."

My son, who loves to be social and hates to sit still, was

in the general education program. *So, he gets to sit at a desk and fill out a packet while the "gifted" kids act out trench warfare?* I thought. That didn't seem fair.

As I took graduate classes and learned strategies for teaching the gifted, I kept thinking, "These aren't strategies to teach just gifted kids—these are good teaching strategies for all kids." Although many teachers I know share this belief, not all do.

Luckily, Jack's elementary school teachers appreciated his strengths. In grades 3–6, he was enrolled in the general education program, and every single teacher he had was amazing. They made learning meaningful and fun, and he loved Ms. Butler, Mrs. Kight, Mr. D, and Ms. Tang! Each of these teachers was able to see in Jack a smart kid with a good sense of humor and a kind heart—so much more important than perfectly imparting the curriculum. Each of these teachers believed in him and, in turn, Jack believed in himself.

The idea that a student's reality can be positively or negatively influenced by the expectation of his teacher is supported by research. In one of my classes, I was struck by the Rosenthal–Jacobson study, which showed that if teachers expected enhanced performance from children, then the children's performance rose—it's the Pygmalion effect in the classroom. "When we expect certain behaviors of others, we are likely to act in ways that make the expected behavior more likely to occur."[3]

Unfortunately, for some, the general education program carries a stigma, and the expected behaviors are not ideal. I recall one high school information night in particular. An English teacher and a History teacher were talking about a combined class they taught. I was enthralled as they spoke about how they worked together to integrate the time period they were studying with the literature they were reading. What a great idea! "We offer this class for our honors sections," one teacher told us.

"This sounds fascinating," I told the teacher. "Would you ever consider offering this class in the general education program?"

"No, those kids are too disruptive," she responded. (*Those* kids? Why did she think I was asking? Did it even occur to her that I had one of *those* kids?)

In some classrooms, there is a real disparity in the quality of education offered to "honors" and "gen ed" students. Maybe that's why I thought I belonged in a general education classroom. I wanted the chance to offer all students a quality education; I wanted my students to know that I expected them to succeed. Maybe that's why I was willing to leave the comfort zone of my great team and known curriculum to make that switch. It might sound crazy, but I felt a strong

---

3 Rosenthal, Robert, and Elisha Y. Babad. "Pygmalion in the Gymnasium," *Educational Leadership* 43, no. 1 (September 1985): 36, http://www.ascd.org/ASCD/pdf/journals/ed_lead/el_198509_rosenthal.pdf.

pull in my heart that gen ed was where I was supposed to be.

Every year, I tell my students, "We'll be learning a new curriculum together. We'll take risks and make mistakes. We'll learn and grow together as a community. We're going to have an amazing year, and I believe in you!"

WHAT DOES THE FOX SAY?

One year, I had a boy in my class who was a bit quirky. He was short for his age, and his parents always seemed to buy his clothes a few sizes too big, maybe hoping they would last longer as he grew into them. The result was that he often looked like he was wearing a dress when his T-shirt fell past his knees.

At first, Max seemed quiet and reserved, and he didn't socialize much with other students in the class. Eventually, I discovered more about his interests. Max loved two things: LEGO sets and singing. Now LEGOs I could understand— they were quite popular with students during indoor recess. But singing? It was hard to imagine this seemingly shy boy singing—until I had a chance to see Max perform one spring afternoon.

The March morning's windy, rainy weather broke into a beautiful day and we all tumbled out of the trailers onto the playground. The teachers sat, as usual, on the bench in the middle of the field to keep watch over their flocks. Max wandered over.

"Guys, I have a song for you," he said.

We turned our full attention to Max. As if onstage, he began to sing Ylvis's 2013 hit song "The Fox (What Does the Fox Say?)"

He started to dance around the bench, all the teachers clapping and cheering as he sang at the top of his lungs. He paused in front of us, more animated than I'd ever seen him, and belted out the chorus.

It was hilarious and heartwarming. The song stayed in my head the rest of the afternoon. I bet the infectious tune stayed with Max as well. Every time I thought of it, I smiled. I think he did too. Does this have anything to do with standardized testing or curriculum? No. But it's moments like these that make teaching worthwhile.

SUPERHEROES DON'T CRY

I didn't cry when I learned I'd be outside in one of the school's trailers (or "the Quad" as we call our set of four) one year because I knew from experience about all the benefits. Being out in the Quad is a bit of a paradox because it both brings people together and keeps people away at the same time.

Working in the Quad is like having roommates again—you can keep the doors open and talk across the classrooms without much effort. Because of this, it's pretty impossible not to become close with your quadmates—and it's good to have close friends (your Quad Squad) because no one else will venture outside the main building to come visit you, ever. Which, honestly, is kind of nice because no one is going to bother you during a tour of the school or a pop-in visit mid-lesson.

As long as I'm describing the superhero headquarters of the Quad Squad, here are some other amazing features: I'd be able to staple anything and everything directly to the walls.

I imagined myself with a holster slung around my hip and one stapler drawn in each hand.

Mrs. Kelly, fastest draw in the Quad!

Also, I would have control over my own thermostat! In the main building, we are subjected to the temperature of the day, which can vary from freezing to sweltering. I used to keep an extra cardigan draped over the back of my chair for options.

Mrs. Kelly, wears a sweater only when she wants to!

Yes, proximity to the bathroom and inclement weather would require planning ahead, but I was already scrolling online for a new pair of rain boots.

Mrs. Kelly with her stylish wellies!

I didn't cry when I learned I would be sharing my classroom with another resource teacher. I get it—after being a classroom teacher for thirteen years, I'd be switching to a new role. I was prepared to be flexible. Lucky for me, my new roomie was also a superhero bundle of energy. She's fun and we worked hard all day Monday to unpack.

Mrs. Kelly, able to transform a massive pile
of furniture, boxes, and crates into a shared
learning community in a single afternoon!

I didn't cry when I learned that, due to last-minute regis-
trations, our room assignment had changed. My roomie and
I were now moving out of our spacious digs into a smaller,
windowless workroom called the Pod. I mean, at least Pod
still rhymes with Squad, right? And being back in the main
building, think of all the money I'd save not shopping for
new rain boots! So, Thursday afternoon we spent repacking
boxes, rolling up our rug, and debating about furniture as we
prepared to downsize. If I had shed a tear, it would have been
for our incredible custodial staff, with superpower strength
and extra thick back braces, who moved an endless supply
of furniture throughout the week. And Friday we spent the
morning unpacking again, making our space happy again.

Mrs. Kelly, able to unpack twice in one week and
still be prepared to welcome students on Monday!

I didn't cry on Friday afternoon when the dust settled
and the boxes were broken down and I could finally turn
my attention to my week ahead. I printed out my list of
students. I picked up my calendar and made the rounds to
teachers, scheduling times to meet with individual students,

join team planning meetings, and visit classrooms. I had a total of ninety-one students to meet scattered among seven different grade levels and twenty-two different classroom teachers—and I was smiling! I couldn't wait to meet all these beautiful faces and begin to build relationships with them. I couldn't wait to learn more about them and decide how to most effectively meet their needs. I was thrilled to work with so many amazing teachers and hoped I could be helpful to them. At our opening kickoff, our superintendent shared a favorite quote, "The main thing is to keep the main thing the main thing," and my main thing is our students.

Mrs. Kelly, able to say "main thing" four times in a single sentence!

So, when I returned to my new happy place with my new roommate and my new schedule, prepared to start my year as a resource teacher, I was unprepared for an email from my principal. "Currently we do not have a teacher for the fourth grade classroom ... we will need you teaching in the fourth grade classroom until we find a teacher or a substitute."

I get it. And, don't get me wrong, I didn't mind. After all, the main thing is our students. One of the things I love about the staff at our school is our sense of collective responsibility—they aren't your students or my students—we all have a stake. I'm happy to help. But after overcoming so many challenges to be prepared for next week, I suddenly felt completely unprepared for next week. On Friday afternoon at 2:30. I didn't feel like a superhero, able to transform from a resource teacher into a fourth grade teacher in a single bound. **And I cried**.

Then I blew my nose in a tissue and went down to visit the fourth grade hallway. I sat with the instructional coach, and she helped me map out a plan for team teaching. Everyone was helpful and thoughtful and kind and patient while my totally unspontaneous mind processed the change.

"I'm sorry I cried," I told my superhero roomie.

"That's okay, I cried earlier when we were packing up for the second time," she told me.

"I'm sorry I cried," I told the teacher across the hall.

"Hey, don't worry. I cry all the time," she responded.

And that's when I realized superheroes do cry. Because we're superhumans and we care about ourselves and others. Just because we're super doesn't mean we're not sometimes disappointed or angry or grieving. Sometimes we use our capes to dry our eyes, and sometimes we use our capes to fly, and sometimes we put our capes in the laundry and have a glass of wine.

So cheers to all my fellow teachers! I know you will take on more than humanly possible and still get it all done. Most important, you will make a difference in the lives of students. Cape or no cape, cry or no cry, that's the main thing.

Part III

Hearth and Home Work

If you have never been hated by your child,
you have never been a parent.

—Bette Davis

FUN CRUSHER

When you are a list maker, planner, goal setter, and time manager like I am, it is sometimes frustrating to live in a house where people don't share these qualities. Especially if these people happen to be your children.

I find this to be most problematic when I try to set goals for these people. Read for thirty minutes a day, make your bed, put your dishes in the dishwasher.

I think I am teaching them to be organized.

The kids think organized = a fastidious, hypercritical, boring, micromanaging perfectionist.

The kids think, "These are all things MOM wants us to do … not things we think are worthwhile uses of our time."

"Ugh, you are such a fun crusher," Jack laments when I ask him to turn off the TV and read first. I feel so discouraged. Shouldn't I be teaching them good habits? Isn't it a part of my parental job description to make sure they are held accountable? How will they succeed if they are so disorganized?

The kids think disorganized = casual, spontaneous,

free-spirited, fun, yay.

It's impossible to enforce the goals I created for my children. Unless I prompt my kids daily and give them multiple reminders, these activities are not completed. And the excuses are endless. Running late to camp—no time to make my bed! Invited to the pool with friends—will read later! Downstairs watching TV—oh yeah, I forgot. Finally in bed with a book—wait, is that your iTouch? Too tired to read—will do it tomorrow.

I battle with my conflicted feelings whenever I offer a reminder.

> Aggravation. *I have to stop what I am doing to remind others of their responsibilities. (I have my own list, people!)*
> Sadness. *They are not intrinsically motivated to do a few simple chores. (Am I raising lazy children?)*
> Resentment. *I am working so hard and they are not helping.*
> Guilt. *I am not being consistent with my parenting guidelines.*

One day, I let them watch TV and put their dishes in the dishwasher for them. The next day I storm downstairs and threaten to cancel Netflix before I even remind them. Will I be Mom Jekyll or Mrs. Hyde today?

I don't know what the answer is, but when they leave for

camp, I see things differently. The beds stay made. There aren't any dirty, crusty bowls down by the TV. The house is quiet. It's then that I forget my frustrations, remembering instead how sweet Jack was when he baked delicious chocolate chip cookies. I forget about the disaster in the craft room and remember Katherine's creativity making original tie-dye socks for a friend. I miss their hugs and snuggles, and I miss them. Maybe they'll forget about my nagging and miss me too.

HAPPY BIRTHDAY! YOU'RE GROUNDED.

I'm in a bit of a pickle. What started as a simple disagreement analyzing the meaning of the phrase "Please turn off the TV now," escalated into a full-blown conflict with Jack on his twelfth birthday. At one point, he left the house and climbed the maple tree in our front yard and I calmly talked him down using my innate intuitive senses and experience with children.

Just kidding. I stood down by the trunk with my neck craned back, looking at the tips of his shoes peeking through the leaves and yelled irrational things like, "If you don't come down right now, you are grounded for four days!"

Has this ever happened to you? In the heat of the moment, you open your mouth and offer a completely unrealistic consequence? Now what?

The pattern in our house is to backpedal. Usually, after a good night's sleep, I realize the punishment does not fit the crime. Then we all hug and say sorry and there ends up being no consequence at all.

Now, I know that grounding a child for four days for climbing a tree is not effective parenting. But neither is giving a consequence and then not following through. So that is my pickle.

I think part of the reason this occurs is that Jack is an amazing kid and we are proud of him in so many ways. His good behavior, kind heart, and happy disposition are the norm, so we end up surprised and unprepared for moments of misbehavior. The twelfth birthday is a milestone because the teenage years are approaching. There will be many mother-son conflicts to come. We would need to sit down together to talk about realistic expectations and consequences. And then I'd need to be consistent and fair in following through. But on that day, I decided to eat my pickle. I told Jack that the punishment was too harsh and asked him to think of a different, more appropriate consequence. 'Cause what mom wants her son to remember the year he was grounded on his birthday?

I'M NOT COMPLAINING, BUT ...

" od loves a cheerful giver. God loves a CHEERFUL giver."
I repeated this to myself over and over as I packed.

Sleeping bag? Check.
Mess kit? Check.
Cheerful outlook? Rats.
Two out of three ain't bad, right?

It's not that I didn't want to spend the weekend chaperoning Katherine's Girl Scout camping trip. Hmmm, well, actually I really didn't want to spend the weekend chaperoning a Girl Scout camping trip. I'd rather stay home.

I did enjoy being a Girl Scout leader. I had the pleasure and privilege of working with a wonderful group of ten-year-olds. But some months we would have an outing every Saturday: a hike to the Billy Goat Trail, a service project raking leaves. How much togetherness did we need?

Oops, I do not sound cheerful, do I?

On that morning, I dreamt of cozying up by the fire reading the paper and drinking coffee from my new coffee maker. Then maybe I'd go to yoga with my friend Debbie and fix myself a big salad for lunch. I imagined myself later in the afternoon turning up some festive Christmas music and fa-la-la-ing as I decked my halls with painted nutcrackers and evergreen wreaths. Paul and I could put our feet up and enjoy a drink together before I whipped up a delicious dinner. Then we'd end the day snuggled on the couch with a family movie.

It cheered me to daydream, but if I were honest with myself, I'd admit that staying home was not likely to be any more relaxing than my chaperoning duties. There would be an early morning basketball game, and Tatum would need a long walk. The giant history project was due Monday, and I was pretty sure it hadn't even been started. Someone needed to buy groceries to prepare for the twenty-one people showing up at our house for the church youth group progressive dinner. We were the salad stop. If the house could be sorta straight and the toilet clean before company arrived, that would be great.

We're not the only parents who seem to sacrifice every weekend to our children's schedules because the kids are in that maniacal age bracket—old enough to be active but too young to drive. After we sign them up for all these activities, we are at their mercy.

I had recently invited a friend over and this was her reply:

We unfortunately have a really crazy weekend. There are swim meets and basketball games and husband and I have a work party to go to Saturday night, which will be very late. Of course now we find out Child 1 has a late baseball game too. Sunday I have a swim meet with Child 2 and baseball game with Child 3. I'd love to come, and thanks for the invite, but I think we will be beat. I hope they don't have tons of homework too.

So that weekend, when I slowed down to consider the alternatives, the camping trip sounded just fine. It was only twenty-four hours of my life, some of which would be spent sleeping. (Yes, sleeping may have been wishful thinking.) We were looking at decent weather—not always guaranteed the first week of December. There would be some creative skits, I'd get to go on a hike, help build a campfire, and even get a s'more or two out of the deal. Best of all, Katherine was thrilled that I was coming.

When I started to think about having a Saturday all to myself, I realized that my Saturdays might soon be spent overseeing the college application process. In a few short years, I'd have all the Saturdays to myself I could want. I remembered that no one is forcing me to be involved in my children's lives. It's a choice that I make gladly, realizing that they grow up too fast.

Water bottle? Check.
Bandanna? Check.
Cheerful outlook? Why not.

DRY SOCKS

It was raining at 6:57 a.m. I knew because I looked out the window before giving Jack an update on the time. "It's 6:57!" I called. Jack's bus comes every day at 7:02 a.m. He is supposed to leave at 6:57 to allow time to walk to the bus stop. Many days he sprints out the door at 7:01. If he misses the bus, he has to walk the mile to school. He hasn't missed the bus yet.

Until today.

"Will you give me a ride?" he asked.

I stood firm. "Sorry, Jack. We have an agreement that you will walk to school if you miss the bus."

"But it's raining," he argued.

"Would you like an umbrella?" I suggested.

Jack retreated into the house, presumably to retrieve an umbrella for our trek. He returned empty handed. "Dad said he'd give me a ride!"

Here's what I wanted to say to Paul at that moment: "Seriously? What happened to consistency? What happened to following through on consequences? What happened to us being on the same page in our parenting decisions? And why, if we're going to play good cop/bad cop, do I have to be the bad cop?"

I didn't say any of those things. I stormed back into the house, grabbed an umbrella, and thrust it into Jack's hands.

The first part of our walk was quiet, except for the gentle patter of rain. Jack was angry and I was stubborn, and we made quite a pair, the two of us. Bundled up in rain jackets, our hoods pulled tightly around our faces, we walked silently side by side. Jack kept the umbrella closed and it swung from his wrist as he moved. Tatum was with us, his soft, thick fur glistening with wetness. The rain began to fall harder, and Jack broke the silence. "Why are you so mean?"

This was a good question and I mulled it over. I don't try to be mean. What, exactly, had I done that was so mean? Is it mean to follow through on a consequence because the weather is not cooperating? Good parenting should always be consistent and reasonable. But what happens when you can't be both? I chose consistent. In hindsight, reasonable might have been the better option.

As we began to climb the hill by the school, we were in the middle of a torrential downpour. The sidewalk was flooding as the rain rushed back down the way we had come. There was nowhere to walk except straight through. My pants were waterlogged and dragging with the extra weight, and my socks and shoes were completely soaked.

"Jack, I'm sorry. I don't try to be mean. I love you and sometimes I think I know what's best for you. In this case, I think I made a mistake. We look like two drowned rats."

Now I was no longer feeling stubborn and Jack was no longer feeling angry. We both just felt cold and really wet. After dropping Jack off, I returned home and packed dry clothes for him. Then I drove up to the school to deliver the bag.

If I could have a "do-over" of that morning, I'm not sure what I would do. Give him a ride? Make him wear rain boots and use his umbrella? Wake him up ten minutes earlier? Parenting decisions aren't often black and white. Sometimes adults make mistakes too. Maybe I wouldn't change our morning. Maybe the real lesson I taught Jack is this:

When you make a mistake, admit your error, say you're sorry, and put on some dry socks.

WHO SCREAMS FOR ICE CREAM?

Three dollars. Two children. One kid scoop each. No whining.

That was our usual Baskin Robbins routine, but this night was different. We were in the car with Sissa and she was treating us all to ice cream! Oh, and did I mention it was 103 degrees out? We were hot, hungry, and ready!

"Can we get two scoops?" Jack asked.

"You can get whatever you want," Sissa replied.

Who knew that phrase could be trouble? Once at Baskin Robbins, the kids noticed the menu board for the first time. So many choices—sundaes, smoothies, scoop sizes, and flavors. Decisions were made and we got in line. Then, at the last minute, Jack changed his mind and ordered a giant Reese's sundae concoction complete with caramel syrup, whipped cream, the works.

Katherine was next ... but suddenly her two-scoop order seemed small and plain compared to her brother's. As the line grew behind her, she looked back up at the menu board in desperation.

"Just get what you planned," I prodded her. "Don't worry about your brother."

"Get the Mega-Oreo Sundae," Jack chimed in. "That looks good."

"That seems like an awful lot of ice cream," I chastised. "I think you should go with your original plan. Just hurry up and decide because people are waiting."

So, Katherine went ahead with her order, but when it arrived she started to cry. In hindsight, of course, I can see how I could have handled this situation differently. I could have been more patient—pulled her out of the line to give her more time to mull over her choices. I could have said, "Oooh, yes! The Mega-Oreo Sundae looks fabulous—yum!"

But who knows? After a long, hot day, Katherine was tired. And, just like her mother, she likes to feel prepared with a plan. Later I talked with my mom about Katherine's meltdown. "What should I do? Is there a way to teach her how to be more spontaneous? I mean, I feel like it's my job as her mother to help her work on this."

"No," Sissa said. "I think it is your job as a mother to show her you love and embrace everything about her. She should feel safe and comfortable coming to you for support—especially when she's tired or cranky."

That advice from my mom permanently changed my view of parenting. Sometimes parenting isn't about being right or imparting a set of rules. It's about showing my kids I love and accept them for who they are. Imperfections and all.

Wow. How'd my mom get to be so smart? I guess she had a lot of practice with me.

TOOLS FOR THE TOOLBOX

"What do you use to get your pushpin into a bulletin board? Probably your thumb. What do you use to put a nail into a 2x4?"

I was talking about tools. Really, I was trying to talk about homework. I would rather NOT talk about homework at all. It is a rather exhausting topic. Jack and I agree on this point. We don't agree on much else, when it comes to homework.

Jack didn't understand his algebra homework, so he decided not to do it. His history assignment was hard and boring, so he decided not to do it. I was trying to convince him that wasn't the answer.

That's where the tool analogy came in. Sometimes, you can't get the job done without the right tools. I was trying to tell him that he had a lot of tools available to him.

The tool of time management: starting homework right after school instead of waiting until bedtime.

The tool of teachers: available for extra assistance if he stayed after school.

The tool of parents: willing to help.

If those aren't enough, we can get a bigger toolbox—work on reading strategies to make history easier or consider medication to help with focus, for instance.

To me, this all seemed perfectly logical. Jack didn't seem to hear any of it. *Wait a minute, are those earbuds peeking out from his sweatshirt? He's not even listening to me. I am the teacher in a Charlie Brown cartoon, "Whaw, whaaw, whawww ..."*

Now I was the one banging my head against a 2x4. I was tired of having the same conversation every week. I looked into my own toolbox:

Tool 1: Try rational argument about the importance of homework. Offer to help. Give a pep talk.

Tool 2: Threaten grounding until Christmas.

Tool 3: Retreat into bedroom in my pajamas with a glass of wine.

Nothing seemed to be the right fit to get the job done. I either needed more wine or new tools. Recognizing this—and understanding that calling wine "homework juice" didn't make it healthy—I decided to try therapy.

I learned a lot about my parenting style in therapy. There's a difference between helping and enabling, and too much helicopter parenting wasn't helping.

"I'm worried he will fail if I don't help," I told my therapist.

"And so what if he does?" she asked me.

Gradually, she helped me understand that Jack perceived my well-meaning meddling as a lack of trust. Slowly, I began to acquire new tools for my toolbox.

Tool 1: Spend quality time together where school topics are off-limits.

Tool 2: Notice strengths rather than pointing out deficiencies.

Tool 3: Let go of the habit of constantly checking on school progress.

Sometimes you can't get the job done without the right tools. Other times, you realize you are not even the carpenter.

ARE YOU THERE, GOD?
IT'S ME, ALLISON.

Dear God,
First of all, thanks a bunch for the torrential
downpour on Monday night.

Someone, somewhere, thought an 8:00 p.m. baseball game in Herndon on a school night was a peachy idea. I, on the other hand, was busy trying to coordinate the completion of algebra homework (for Jack), dance class (for Katherine), and identification profile assessment for grad class (for myself).

Meanwhile it dawned on me that I had not yet a) walked Tatum (*And has he eaten dinner? Wait, did anyone even feed him breakfast?*); b) cooked dinner (*Beanie Weenies again, dear family?*); or c) done the laundry since Jack's last baseball game (*How much do you want to bet his uniform is in a sweaty rumpled pile at the bottom of the hamper?*).

And then, just as I was on the verge of losing any and all remaining sanity, the precipitation began.

I knew it was you, God, sending a storm. A storm outside to cancel the game. An extra gift of time to help calm the storm inside. Thank you.

Second, I am really sorry I've been so bad about talking to you lately. You know these last few months have been crazy busy with me teaching and taking this grad class. I really don't know what I was thinking with the grad class, by the way. And helping Jack and Katherine with homework.

And Girl Scouts.

And baseball.

Sometimes I would wake up at 4:00 a.m. and couldn't fall back to sleep thinking about everything and hoping I wouldn't forget anything. (I told Paul I felt like I needed to cover my whole body with sticky note reminders. Paul said he'd love to see my body covered with nothing but sticky notes. Not sure he got my point.)

Friends kept asking, "How's it going?" The truth was, despite the stress I was under, I had a lot to be thankful for. I loved my class and my team. My days flew by in a sleep-deprived, adrenaline-fueled frenzy. I felt challenged, needed, and appreciated. Every day someone made me laugh. Every day someone made my heart swell with warmth. My class, though a bucketload of work, was stimulating and thought-provoking. Life was far from perfect—I hadn't figured out how to fit in exercise, cooking, or cleaning. But I knew we'd settle into a routine soon enough.

Meanwhile, God, I just wanted to touch base. Every day I am thankful for so many things and, even though I haven't stopped to tell you lately, I really appreciate all of them. Especially the rain.

RECALCULATING

Before I had a smartphone, I owned a GPS named Greta. Sometimes I imagined she had feelings. Greta was like the fifth family member on car trips and was proud of her role as navigator on our excursions. I detected an edge to her voice when we deviated from her suggested routes.

"When possible, make a legal U-turn," she would snap at me. When I ignored her, she seemed to sigh.

"Recalculating," she would mutter in resignation.

The week Jack was invited to join a travel baseball team, I felt a little like Greta. Practice four days a week and games two days a week? Traveling every other weekend for three months? Would we ever eat dinner as a family again? I added up the costs of team fees, equipment, and travel expenses. So much for our patio furniture budget. As the news sunk in about what this new commitment would mean for our family, I wanted to shout, "Whenever possible, make a legal U-turn!"

When Jack had contacted the coach, I'd been impressed with his initiative. When he'd practiced with the team, I'd admired his determination.

When he was invited to join, I panicked.

Slowly, though, I began to process the news. I remembered what a positive experience it would be for Jack to be a part of a team. I considered that his afternoons and weekends might be spent outside in the fresh air instead of down in our basement binge-watching Netflix. I remembered that his grades improved when he was playing a sport—somehow, he managed his free time better when he had less of it.

Recalculating …

One weekend we went to a tournament in Rehoboth Beach. One of my favorite moments was watching Jack sprint to left field and dive across the grass to catch a line drive to the gap. Later the coach said, "One game highlight was Jack's absolute running, horizontal layout. When the ball was hit, I said, 'Uh oh,' and thought no possible way. The effort shown on that one play sent a reverberation through the team."

I never thought I'd be spending a long holiday weekend at a baseball tournament. Sometimes life takes us on a different route than we planned.

MAKE GOOD CHOICES

"The butterfly effect is very interesting," Pop Pop told us as he heaped a serving of potatoes onto his plate.

"I've heard of that," Katherine chimed in. "It's the idea that a butterfly flapping its wings could alter the path of a hurricane."

You never know what the topic of conversation might be when you visit with Pop Pop. One day it's quantum physics, the next day it's baseball. Today we are discussing the butterfly effect, in which small changes in initial conditions can lead to big and unpredictable results.

The days leading up to my kids' departure for college were full of "lasts." The last family dinner night, last night in their own beds, last big hugs for mom—all these activities took on special significance.

Then came the "firsts," such as stepping into the dorm room for the first time, eating the first meal on campus, making the first new friends. There were firsts for Paul and me too—the first time pulling back into the empty driveway was a hard one for sure—until we got the first text reassuring us that our college student was going to be okay.

Before they left, I told my kids, as I often do, "Make good choices. I love you." This isn't the first or last time they would hear that. I thought about what those words mean to me, and what I hope they mean to Jack and Katherine.

1. Choose to be kind to everyone.
2. Choose to be a leader. Use your gifts, talents, and strengths to make a positive impact.
3. Choose to set high standards for yourself. Never miss a class. Never miss a practice.
4. Choose to study. Be curious about the world.
5. Choose to connect with God.
6. Choose to own up to and take responsibility for your mistakes.
7. Choose your friends wisely. You become like those you hang around. Choose friends who also make good choices.
8. Choose to stay healthy and active. Make time to exercise. Say no to drugs.
9. Choose to reframe problems as challenges and lessons.
10. Choose to be thankful.

The daily choices we make aren't usually major decisions but rather tiny flutters, like the wings of a butterfly. It's not what we do once in a while that shapes our lives, but the small choices we make every day. There's so much in our lives that is beyond our control. Being thoughtful about the choices you can control makes it easier to live a life that aligns with your core values.

I miss my kids when they are away, but I am excited about the new opportunities that college offers. I'm proud to see the good choices they are making as they continue to grow and learn. Whether they know it or not, with every choice they make, they flutter their wings and make a difference in the lives of others.

Part IV

Sick Days and Other Ailments

Tis healthy to be sick sometimes.

—Henry David Thoreau

SMOKE ALARMS AND FLIP FLOPS

O ne day, I decided to try taking the day off. By "off," I mean going to physical therapy, making school sub plans, visiting the eye doctor, swinging by the bank, getting the car's oil changed, making a grocery run, cleaning the house, responding to work emails, doing a few loads of laundry, unloading the dishwasher, taking Katherine to the dentist, carpooling for cross country practice, cooking dinner, cleaning the kitchen, and planning the next day's lessons. It felt SO GOOD!

Attempting to balance teaching and parenting isn't new to me, but as much as I try to prepare, each year's challenges are unique. One year, I had twenty-nine amazing fifth graders to love. The good news: to help support all the different levels and learning styles, our class qualified for two special education teachers and an ESOL teacher. The bad news: these three positions had yet to be filled.

I was spending a lot of time trying to balance work and home, and I was getting distracted thinking about it all. At physical therapy I hopped on the treadmill to run and realized I was wearing flip flops. I tried to get a jump-start on dinner by roasting a chicken before breakfast. I opened the oven and a huge poof of smoke came billowing out. *Please don't set off the smoke alarm*, I thought as I frantically fanned the cloud.

Beeeeeeep. Beeeeeep. Too late.

When Paul ran out to the kitchen at 6:00 a.m. to find me in my PJs waving dishtowels in the air, I could only turn, smile, and say, "Dinner's ready!"

I remember when one of my teammates returned to work for the first time since having a baby. It was not easy. "I just feel like a failure," she mentioned as she stuffed her bag full of papers that needed grading. "I don't understand how everyone else does this."

Pssst—here's our secret. We don't. We try, but we end up burning chicken and running in flip flops. We make choices and we prioritize. Sometimes that means eating Fritos and a candy bar for dinner so we're not late to our son's game. Sometimes it means falling asleep at 8:00 p.m. instead of folding laundry. We support each other and we laugh and we drink too much coffee and too much wine. We lose ourselves in the moments that really matter—with our students, our families, our friends.

And sometimes we take a sick day to stay healthy.

HAPPY CRYING

One rough week, I found myself crying. Happy, sad, cathartic ... a whole week's worth of craziness released in sobs and sniffles.

That Sunday I'd discovered I had lice. I found this out when a bug fell out of my head. I teach in an elementary school, so it is probably a small miracle that this was my first (and hopefully last?) bout with the little critters. I spent most of Sunday afternoon quarantined in my bathroom with a bottle of RID shampoo and a nit comb.

On Monday, I spent the day sitting at my desk talking to parents. I don't mind parent-teacher conferences, but they are emotionally draining. I know from the parent's perspective how important it is to feel my children are in the right hands. So I must be "on" all day: answering questions, calming anxious feelings, explaining a quarter's worth of progress in twenty short minutes per family multiplied by twenty-six families.

Tuesday, I had a dentist appointment. Luckily, I always see the same wonderful hygienist named Diane who knows all about my anxieties. When I got to the office, the hygienist came out to greet me. She did not look like Diane at all. She told me her name and then said some other stuff, but I didn't hear her because a voice in my head was screaming, "What the HELL?? You are not DIANE!!"

Person Who is Not Diane led me to a room to take a panoramic x-ray, and I started to feel really claustrophobic, but she was being nice and I was trying to keep it together, so she didn't realize how anxious I was. So, it was really embarrassing when Person Who Is Not Diane said, "You doin' okay?" and I burst into tears.

Luckily, Person Who Is Not Diane was just as nice as Diane, and she made out like, "No big deal, girlfriend. People always bust out crying at the dentist and this is totally normal and you are not at all a giant nutcase."

I know she really thought I was a giant nutcase, but it was awfully nice of her to pretend otherwise.

By Wednesday I felt pretty run-down and had lost my voice. I knew I was going to have to call in sick since talking is pretty much essential for teaching.

So what did I do for my sick day that Thursday? I spent the morning in bed reading *Wonder* and drinking hot tea. It is such a good book, and I won't spoil it for you, but I spent the last quarter of the book crying my eyes out.

The thing is, I wasn't sad. The crying was a release of the week's stress combined with an appreciation for my life— my beautiful, wonderful, crazy, imperfect life—and all the wonderful people who love me.

One of the characters in the book plays Emily in Thorton Wilder's play *Our Town*. With appreciation for the simple joys of life, she says, "Good-by to clocks ticking and Mama's sunflowers. And food and coffee. And new-ironed dresses and hot baths ... and sleeping and waking up. Oh, earth, you're too wonderful for anybody to realize you!"[4]

That's the way I feel sometimes. Life is complicated and messy and, yes, sometimes difficult. But it is also too wonderful for anybody to realize. That's what makes it so amazing.

---

4 R. J. Palacio, *Wonder* (New York: Random House Children's Books, 2017), 231.

CANCER SUCKS

I had surgery to remove skin cancer from my face. So, that was fun.

Just kidding, it wasn't fun at all.

To be honest, I tried to downplay this surgery in the weeks leading up to the procedure. People have more difficult things to deal with than an outpatient appointment and a few stitches.

Whenever I face a challenge, I try to remember James 1:2: "Consider it pure joy, my brothers and sisters, whenever you face trials of many kinds, because you know that the testing of your faith produces perseverance." I mean, I can't say I was feeling joyous about the whole thing, but I definitely felt lucky to have access to early detection and good medical care. I joked that having stitches around Halloween was perfect timing.

On the day of my surgery, Paul drove me to my appointment. Even though it was outpatient, I was a little nervous and was thankful to have the company and a hand to hold in the waiting room. The surgeon numbed the area and then removed the cancerous tissue from the edge of my nose down toward my lip. He cauterized the area (nothing like the smell of burning flesh to remind you to wear sunscreen!) and then examined it in the lab to ensure the margins were cancer free. Next, he returned to stitch up the incision and send me home with instructions to wear the bandage for seven days and avoid exercising, stooping, lifting, and drinking alcohol.

I thought that would be the worst part, but I was wrong. I think that's because I was prepared for the surgery, but I didn't realize what the recovery would be like. I didn't realize it would hurt to laugh, talk, or chew because of where the stitches were located. I didn't foresee how glaring the bandage would look and that it would start to curl up around the edges and smell funny. I didn't think about how self-conscious I would be about returning to work with a giant bandage on my face. Or that not exercising/lifting/stooping for a week would make me feel useless. I didn't think I would start obsessing about every age spot, freckle, or mole on my body, wondering, *Is this normal?* Or that I would worry about the scar and how prominent it would be on my face.

Have you ever bitten the inside of your cheek? And then it sticks out a little so you end up biting it again and again? My recovery was like that. It started to make me feel depressed, and then I felt guilty for being depressed over some stupid, small cancer on my face that wasn't even there anymore. *Come on, Allison. What about James 1:2? Get it together!*

There's actually a name for this. Brené Brown calls it *unwanted identity* when we take on characteristics that undermine our vision of our ideal selves. So, if you think of yourself as healthy and independent, being sick and dependent on others is frustrating.

Intermingled with my self-pity was a renewed appreciation for my life. Friends gave me a get-well gift and I cried with gratitude at their generosity. Family called to check on me. Paul was my rock and loved me through every step of the emotional roller coaster.

And so, the days passed, and the bandage came off. If I wear a little concealer now, you can barely see the scar. It's a part of who I am. I don't mind seeing it in the mirror in the mornings because it's a reminder that we are all less than perfect and that we all have some scars.

TENNIS ELBOW

I've got a bona fide case of tennis elbow. The good news: it is not impacting my tennis game AT ALL! This may be because I don't play tennis ... but I digress. This isn't really about tennis; it's about keeping a budget.

Yes, there are many benefits to being a teacher, but "more money" is not one of them. At first, we tried to get by without a budget. We're not extravagant spenders and we rarely go out to eat. How hard could it be? For a month I tracked our income and expenses to get a baseline of our unchecked spending. Guess what I discovered? We needed a budget.

I could argue that September has some unique expenses— school supplies, gym uniforms, new shoes, school fundraisers—but every month it's always something, isn't it? I looked at our receipts to see where we could make some adjustments and tweak our spending habits. In an effort to reduce our grocery bills, I found myself at the bulk store.

Shopping at the bulk store has the potential to save money, but it takes effort. First, I had to learn to cut coupons, which can be time-consuming but rewarding. Next, I realized that I must buy only what I **know** we will use. The bulk dry pasta for $1.00 per lb. is a good deal, but the bulk box of Chocolate Cheerios that Katherine really, really wanted got stale in the pantry. I also got in the habit of comparing the cost of staples. A gallon of milk at the bulk store was a whopping 96 cents less than the price at the grocery store.

As I budgeted, I also learned to be careful. Who knew saving money could be dangerous? Developing the tennis elbow was a rookie mistake—I tried to pick up a 12-pack of canned soup with one hand while carrying jumbo-sized laundry detergent in the other.

Then there was the coffee bag incident.

I usually buy a small bag of good, quality coffee. When I bought a giant bag of bulk coffee, it was too big for the shelf in my pantry. I poured some of the new coffee into the small empty bag and stored the rest in the freezer. When my mom visited, she didn't know my new system. She used up the coffee and unknowingly threw away a perfectly good empty coffee bag!

The danger came when I told her what happened. After she returned home, she mailed me an empty coffee bag. However, the post office intervened. When my mail arrived, the envelope had been sliced open and the contents inspected. Apparently, coffee grounds are sometimes used to disguise the scent of illegal substances from sniffer dogs. I wondered what the postal inspector thought when he opened a bag that smelled like coffee and found … a coffee bag. Luckily, we avoided the SWAT team descending on our house for a drug raid.

Despite the dangers of being on a budget, I persevered. I've continued to shop at the bulk store … and I always allow time to ice my elbow after.

PANDEMIC GOALS

Do you remember that feeling of distraction when there's an impending blizzard approaching? There's energy in the air and no one can quite concentrate on long division or the causes of the American Revolution because any minute those big flakes are going to start falling. It's pretty much impossible to think about grading papers when you've got to stock up on toilet paper and wine.

That's the way I was feeling in March of 2020, only it was a global pandemic on my mind rather than a weather forecast. Instead of shovels and ice melt, stores ran out of hand sanitizer and Clorox wipes. I was in uncharted territory, full of unsettling unknowns. The coronavirus (COVID-19) impacted each of us in a personal way. Whether dealing with the disappointment of cancelled plans, worrying about the health of a loved one, or feeling scared about the economic consequences, we each felt a significant ripple effect.

None of this was convenient. None of this was planned. And for a list-making, calendar-loving planner like me, that's a recipe for anxiety. And yet, that's how life works. Winston Churchill is credited as having said, "A pessimist sees the difficulty in every opportunity; an optimist sees the opportunity in every difficulty."[5] As schools around the country shut down, I contemplated how to make the most of my time working from home. Maybe I could master a fancy cooking technique or learn how to play the banjo.

Despite my good intentions, I felt myself wandering the house in an unproductive daze. As the days turned to weeks, I was missing structure. Eventually, the weeks turned into months and I still hadn't learned how to play an instrument or make macarons. Instead, I decided to have a sense of humor about my malaise. To lighten the mood, I gave each day a theme.

> *Manic Monday*: Mondays are the perfect day to panic when you realize there's another full week ahead of you. I like to take an inventory of my dwindling supply of toilet paper and do the math to see how many days' worth we have left. Peeking in my pantry is another fun activity to raise anxiety. I wonder what I can whip up with olives and bulgur wheat.

> *Try-again Tuesday*: On Tuesdays, I look at the list of productive ideas I made and wonder what the

---

5 "Winston Churchill Quotes," Brainy Quote, accessed October 19, 2020, www.brainyquote.com/quotes/winston_churchill_103739.

heck I did all day yesterday and why I didn't make time to DO any of these? And then I remember that counting the olives in the jar did take up a substantial part of my day. Tuesday is a much better day to start my replica of the space shuttle made entirely out of toothpicks.

What-day-is-it Wednesday: I feel like Bill Murray in *Groundhog Day*. "I Got You Babe" is playing on the bedside clock radio and I have no idea what day it is. Since every day feels like Blursday, I like to write "Figure out what day it is" on my list of things to do. Once I figure out it's Wednesday, I know what day it is AND I can cross something off my list. Knowledge and productivity! It's a win-win!

Thrifty Thursday: On Thursdays I like to find a DIY project to save a little money. Who needs a professional haircut when you've got a pair of purple scissors in your school box?

Freshen-up Friday: Usually, I figure out it's Friday by giving my armpits the old sniff test. Whew, it must be time for a shower. Sometimes I go a little crazy and put on jeans and a T-shirt instead of leggings and a bathrobe. It's the weekend—a girl's gotta live a little! Come to think of it, it might be time to wash the bathrobe too.

Same-day Saturday: Surprisingly, my Saturdays now look very similar to Saturdays in my old life. The pandemic hasn't put a pause on my weekend chores. I like to give myself little challenges, like can I clean the entire kitchen with one-third of a Clorox wipe? I reward myself with some mindless drivel on Netflix when I'm done.

Sleep-in Sunday: After exerting myself and binge-watching too much Netflix, Sunday is the perfect day to sleep in and recharge. We've got a full week ahead!

There were still days I felt as if a milk crate of books was pressing down on my lungs. Learning how to teach virtually was humbling and overwhelming. I read articles reminding me that stress and anxiety are normal emotions during a pandemic and made a conscious effort not to numb my discomfort with too much wine or online shopping. Instead, I tried healthier ways to cope with the uncertainty and challenges—keeping a gratitude journal, cooking family meals, and trying to keep my sense of humor—no matter what day it was.

Part V

Holidays

We do not remember days, we remember moments.

—Cesare Pavese

SNOW DAY: A WASHINGTON, DC, DEFINITION

snow day (noun): a day on which public schools or other institutions are closed due to heavy snow.

—World English Dictionary

Maybe that's the case in other areas of the country. In the Washington, DC, region, we might need our own definition. The weather in our area is notoriously difficult to predict. Or so the weather forecasters tell me every time they get it wrong.

A **Washington, DC, snow day** (noun) develops a few days in advance with lots of media hype and large-scale projections, "up to a foot of snow possible in some areas...." Clever people always name Washington, DC, snowstorms so we can talk about the impact of "Snowpocalypse" or "Snowquester" on our day, the economy, the power lines, etc. The hype and anticipation are a big part of the ritual because we never know which way the wind will blow (literally) and how it will ultimately affect us. Kids (and teachers) share their expert, foolproof ways to bring on the snow—wearing inside-out pajamas, putting spoons under the pillow, dropping ice cubes in the toilet, choreographing snow dances. We haven't had significant snow in our area in a while, so "We want a snow day!" is a popular refrain.

In the early morning hours on the day of the approaching storm, Washington, DC, snow day hype continues. I don't envy the people who have to make the decision to close schools and government buildings in our area. Using information they receive from the completely unreliable meteorologists, they decide our fates. Err on the side of caution and hear the ridicules and complaints. Take a gamble and risk eight-hour commuting gridlock calamity. Most days, they err on the side of caution. I don't blame them. I'd take ridiculing over a traffic jam any day of the week.

No school! A Washington, DC, snow day really begins after the announcement is posted. Snow days mean sleeping in late. Drinking coffee and reading by the fire. Putting on the snow pants, boots, mittens, hats, coats, and heading out into the … hmm. Where's the snow?

A Washington, DC, snow day is a day subject to ridicule. "Snowquester" changes to "Slushquester" when most of our area gets rain. Residents recently transplanted from the North and Midwest shake their heads in disbelief. **Washington, DC, sprinkler day**, anyone?

Yeah, the fluffy white stuff would have been nice. But I'll take the extra day off anyway. Washington, DC, snow day works for me. No snow required.

LUCKY

For the Kelly family, March is the time to celebrate one of our favorite holidays: St. Patrick's Day. Just turning the calendar page causes Paul to start reciting limericks in his Irish accent. It's his cue to start planning his menu of shepherd's pie and a Guinness (or two) to celebrate.

I haven't found any four-leaf clovers or chased any leprechauns over the rainbow to a pot of gold ... yet. That's okay because I am already lucky—I married my Irish good luck charm. I really should tell him how wonderful he is more often.

Paul, how'd I get so lucky?

You take care of me. Before I go for a bike ride, you put the air in my tires and attach the bike rack to my car.

You are always complimenting my cooking. Even when it looks like glob. You tell me it's the best glob you've ever eaten. And then you clean the kitchen after I cook. Sometimes I leave an awful mess. You've scrubbed your fair share of pots.

When you're reading the newspaper, you don't mind when I interrupt you to comment on the article I'm reading. Or you pretend not to mind. That makes me happy.

You go to the grocery store for me. Even when you are tired. Even when it is rush hour. And you never complain about it.

I love to hear you sing and play the guitar. I'm glad we have common interests like riding bikes, running, listening to live music, reading good books, and eating good food.

You are a wonderful writer, and I cherish the poems and notes you write. I love that you leave the kids notes on their lunchbox napkins.

Speaking of kids, you are the best dad ever. When I watched you teaching Katherine how to swing a tennis racquet, I knew she would forever keep her eye on the ball and follow through on her forehand. I love seeing you spend time dribbling the basketball in our driveway as you shoot hoops with Jack.

And did I mention you are the most handsome man ever?

Most important, you love me. You love everything about me. Even my imperfections. And I love you.

Paul, how'd I get so lucky?

HAPPY BIRTHDAY, JOHNNY APPLESEED

Big holidays stress me out. Every year I swear I will not be overwhelmed by the holiday preparations, and every year I succumb to the idea of what this holiday "should" look like. That's why I prefer the spontaneity of celebrating a minor holiday. There are no preconceived notions, it requires less prep work, and it's a lot more fun. For example, Johnny Appleseed's birthday.

Johnny Appleseed (his real name was John "the Worm" Chapman) was an American pioneer who spent fifty years traveling the Midwest. He created apple orchards in Illinois, Indiana, Kentucky, Pennsylvania, and Ohio. Some of those trees still bear apples to this day. (Okay, you got me. I made up "the Worm." But everything else is true. I think.)

It is hard to know for sure because there are many stories about Johnny Appleseed in American folklore. Some say he wore a tin pot on his head and walked around barefoot. In one story, a rattlesnake tries to bite Johnny's foot but the fangs can't puncture his thick skin. Johnny is known as being friendly and kind, even to animals. In another tale, he dances with bears.

Maybe some of the stories are exaggerated, but so what? Johnny still seems like a great guy and one worth celebrating. And so, we decided to go for it one year. Katherine donated her expert party planning skills. For the table setting, she made apple napkin rings and our centerpiece was a row of shiny red apples.

Then we invited some guests to the party. Pop Pop and Uncle Stu were happy to participate. We sang the Johnny Appleseed grace and dined on oven-fried chicken, succotash, biscuits, and applesauce. And, of course, there was apple pie for dessert. Uncle Stu even brought the ice cream.

After dinner we tested our knowledge of John Chapman's life with a little trivia game. Pop Pop declared himself the winner, but I suspect there might have been a little creative point totaling because I thought I was the Amazing Apple Trivia Queen. Good food and fun times with family. Thanks, Johnny Appleseed, for giving us an excuse to celebrate.

<u>The Johnny Appleseed Grace</u>[6]
Oh, the Lord is good to me
And so I thank the Lord
For giving me
The things I need
The sun and the rain and the apple seed
The Lord is good to me.

---

6 This is the version I learned in Girl Scouts and sang as a grace before meals as a kid.

AHEAD OF THE CURVE

Hey, you, with the pumpkin. Put that down. Don't you know it's October? You've got to get started on Christmas. I carved my jack-o'-lantern back in August and, I gotta tell you, it is looking really scary right now.

What? You're busy with fall foliage and football? I was once like you, my friend, waiting until my turkey and pecan pie were long digested before I gave any thought to fa-la-la-ing. But I learned my lesson one December after reading two simple words on a storefront sign: Clearance Sale.

The craft store advertisement caught my eye in mid-December. I had been thinking about hanging wreaths from my windows, having always admired the classic, festive adornments on the homes of others. With wreaths priced at 50% off, I decided to dress up the facade of my own house. I braved the traffic for a trip to the strip mall and headed toward the store in anticipation and excitement.

I was picturing the finished scene in my mind—maybe I could use some plaid ribbons to hang the wreaths. And, of course, I would add a cheerful, lush red bow on each one. Then Paul could hook up a few flood lamps to spotlight the windows. Oh! Maybe I'd add a candle to rest on each sill. Ideas were still multiplying as I stepped inside the store. Abruptly, the joyful vision in my mind was replaced with the scene before me. It was utter chaos.

Advent, as in the season of advent, literally means "to prepare." The liturgical calendar tells us we have four weeks to get organized for Christmas. The staff at Michaels does not share this view. In their opinion, shopping in mid-December puts you waaaay behind the curve. They had their holiday stuff out in October, people! Where had we been? The smart customers had snapped up their shopping bargains on Black Friday and Cyber Monday. Lights had been shimmering on their evergreens and rooftops since Thanksgiving.

Those of us braving the store that day were the hapless fools, lured in by the promise of savings. With Christmas still almost two weeks away, we were labeled procrastinators. And let me tell you, the early birds got all those worms weeks ago. Gone were the candles. Gone were the lights. And gone were the red velvety bows. All that was left were some gaudy plastic poinsettias and a Charlie Brown tree made in China.

By mid-December, these folks were done with Christmas. The reason they were having a Clearance Sale, people, was so they could clear their store of all this unwanted merchandise to make room for Valentine's Day crafts.

Undeterred, I poked around the half-bare shelves and

managed to find a few wreaths. The bows would have to wait. All they had left were a few faded maroon ones, which I left for another customer's buying pleasure.

As traumatizing as that shopping experience was, I learned my lesson. Fast-forward to the next October. I passed by a neighbor's home decked out for Halloween: pumpkins by the doorstep, window clings of black cats and skeletons on display through the glass, and tattered ghosts blowing from the tree branches. *Suckers*, I thought. Blissfully unaware, they were busy enjoying a beautiful fall day.

I knew better. I was heading to the land of holly and jolly, where the lawn reindeer beckon and the ornaments sparkle. I've heard the red bows are in abundance this time of year.

COFFEE POTS AND MARRIAGE

My coffee maker used to drive me crazy. An obscure brand, I bought it on sale when our old one broke. The pouring spout was curled around the lip, so when I tipped it, the coffee would cling to the edge of the pot and trickle down the side, leaving a puddle on the counter. I would gauge the success of my pour by the number of paper towels it took to clean up.

In the spirit of reducing our paper towel usage, my dear wonderful husband decided to surprise me with a new, beautiful, deluxe coffee maker.

I hate it.

Our new appliance has a stainless steel pot. While its opaque finish may be aesthetically pleasing, I have no way of measuring the amount of water in the pot as I fill it. In addition, its insulated lining means a smaller capacity than our old model. Not as practical for serving company, I think, as the holidays approach. Worst of all is the coffee itself, if that's what you want to call it. More like brown hot water.

Staring down into my steaming mug, I mulled over my dilemma. *If I act grateful for a gift I don't like, I will have to drink this excuse for coffee every morning indefinitely. If I tell the truth, I risk hurting Paul's feelings. I risk giving him the message that he is not helpful and should just leave the errands to me.*

I decided to be patient. "Sweetie, I am having trouble with the new coffee maker. I'm not sure I'm using it correctly. Could you please try making a pot?"

I watched as Paul carefully measured the grounds. I watched as he poured in the water. After it brewed, he poured himself a cup of coffee and took a sip. I noticed his nose wrinkle up a little. "Hmm, seems a bit weak," he said.

"Yes," I agreed. I decided to point out the coffee maker's other deficiencies and then I looked at Paul. He was crest-fallen. Oh no, I'd hurt his feelings!

"Well, I guess I just shouldn't try to do errands for you," he lamented.

I put down my coffee mug and gave him a big hug. "Honey, this coffee pot is not perfect. But you are perfect for me. I love you."

Later that year, Paul and I celebrated our fifteen-year wedding anniversary. In a card from his parents, his father wrote:

Marriage, mirroring life, generally is not a series of ongoing earth-shaking events. Rather, it is the ordinary day-to-day routine in which we are given

the opportunity to piece together a mosaic of little
special happenings into a beautiful picture.

Most days, nothing earth-shaking happens to me. I go to work and walk the dog. I return a coffeemaker and choose a new one. It's probably not perfect either. It will break someday as well. But as long as I'm able to drink my coffee with Paul, it's perfect for me.

A CASE OF THE CHRISTMAS GIGGLES

There was a big black hole in the middle of my Christmas tree one year. Now, I'm not too bad when it comes to lights—I always check the bulbs before I string them, and I rarely make that rookie mistake of winding them the wrong way, ending up with nothing to plug into the outlet. That year's light-stringing went without a hitch and the tree looked great … at first.

"What happened to the tree?" Katherine asked. What happened indeed. Apparently, one string went out. Of course, it was the string right in the middle of the tree. Have you ever tried to unwind a light string from an already decorated tree? Neither have I. And I wasn't about to start.

As long as I'm pointing out imperfections, the stockings were not hung by my chimney with care. I affixed them with push pins. We were having company in about two hours and I hadn't started cooking dinner yet. The floor wouldn't be mopped, and I'd scratched the idea of homemade dessert long ago in favor of store-bought pie. So, it wouldn't be perfect, but that was okay.

I think about Mary's plan for the birth of Jesus. I'm pretty sure her Lamaze coach, the midwife, and the doula would not have recommended the cramped, smelly, unsanitary manger as their top choice for the big event. Yet, even in less-than-ideal circumstances, Mary gave birth to a perfect baby.

One Christmas when I was little, my grandparents gave our family the gift of a tape player and a tape of Christmas songs. Remember mix tapes? I used to make them all the time when I was a kid. After recording a new masterpiece, I would take a ballpoint pen and poke out the little plastic tab on the side of the tape to make my creation permanent. This mix tape was, apparently, recorded at home in some lady's basement. We could tell. Along with the novice production, the singing was not much better. The lady had a warbly and at times screechy voice.

At first my brother and I were disappointed. This was not the perfect Christmas gift we had imagined. The tape probably would have been cast aside except for one thing: Bobby and I discovered the little plastic tab still intact on the side of the tape. This was a perfectly good cassette! We could dub over the entire thing!

We hit the play button and listened to the piano plinking and plunking as the lady sang with dramatic flourish.

"And the angels ..." she crooned. Quickly we hit record and updated the lyrics with our own childlike melody.

" … laughed so hard they wet their pants!"

And then we laughed so hard that we almost wet our pants. We spent hours with our new gift that afternoon. Lying on our stomachs on the living room carpet, we rewrote the words to every song and inserted our new, improved version onto the tape.

So, our tree may have some dark spots from time to time, but our home will always be full of the light and laughter of good friends. And maybe a Christmas carol or two. I know one about angels … that sounds just perfect to me.

HAPPY BIRTHDAY TO ME

There's a black hole between Christmas and New Year's when no one seems to know what day it is, we're feeling sluggish from too many cookies, and we've reached our capacity on family togetherness. So, who wants to celebrate my birthday?

I used to resent having been born during this window between Christmas and New Year's. Amid holiday hustle and bustle, company, activities, and entertaining, I felt my birthday wasn't special enough—too easily forgotten. And since we were home for break, I never got to bring cupcakes to share with my class like the other kids in school.

In fact, for a period of my life, I changed my birthday. A few friends still laugh about the time I announced I had moved my birthdate to January 29—sharing the date with my best friend from high school.

Now older, and maybe even a little wiser, I welcome the benefits of my special day. One advantage is having the space to take a little "alone time" during our winter recess without feeling selfish. I love having the kids home, my husband home, and the grandparents and aunts and uncles and presents and cookies and adventures—I really do. I spend extra time cooking, playing new board games, and curling up with Paul to watch old TV shows. As much as I adore it all, though, being off my regular schedule for too long wears me out. I like to use my birthday as an excuse to clear my head. In the morning I exercise, working up a great sweat for the first time all week. I might normally feel guilty leaving all morning but, hey, it's my birthday!

I return to dine with my family on the meal of my request—a big healthy salad. I open presents and receive my annual birthday phone call from my mother. "That morning I woke up complaining of gas pains. So your father says, 'Well, how far apart are these gas pains?'"

After lunch, I pamper myself with a pedicure and redeem a free cup of birthday coffee. I find a comfy spot to savor my latte and pull out the spiral notebook I had stashed in my bag. I have come to appreciate my birthday's location on the calendar. The fifty-second and last week of the year is a good time to take stock of myself—to reflect on all that happened during the past year and to look ahead to the next.

Journal, check.
Toenails, check.
Yoga, check.

After refreshing my mind, body, and spirit, I return home.

One special year we welcomed guests: my dear friend Kristin and her family. Because it was winter break, the whole clan made the trip—a luxury I wouldn't have on just any Thursday during the year. We got caught up, relaxed, laughed. It was all so comfortable. We feasted on Lebanese carryout served on paper plates, saving room for Steve's famous homemade chocolate peanut butter cake. The adults lingered at the table talking while the girls rehearsed silly birthday skits.

As the festivities came to an end, I got one last Happy Birthday hug and kiss from my pajama-clad family before I nestled beneath the covers.

That's what I call a wonderful birthday. I wouldn't have it any other way on any other day.

Part VI

Extracurricular Activities

Do one thing every day that scares you.

—Eleanor Roosevelt

TURTLE GIRLS

The turtle sensed I was approaching before I saw her. Did she see me? Could she feel the vibrations of my bicycle on the asphalt? I wasn't sure. As I crested the hill, there she was in the middle of the street. It was early Sunday morning, so I hadn't yet seen anyone out and about. Still, I worried. I rode past her down the hill, enjoying my break from pedaling, and rounded the corner past my house to start the loop again.

I was out early on the bike because my dear friend Kristin had talked me into doing a triathlon with her to celebrate her fortieth birthday. I rode up the other side of my neighborhood and back to the hill with the turtle. She had made a little progress since I last saw her. *Why did the turtle cross the road?* I thought with a smile.

I thought the triathlon would force me to be more adventurous. Instead, I worried. I worried about swimming in a crowded pool. I worried about biking on a road open to traffic. I worried about the heat in August. And now, I was worrying about a turtle.

I haven't always been so uptight and anxious. When Kristin and I met, life was an adventure and we were invincible spirits. I'm not sure what happened to our adventurous spirits. We grew up, became mothers. Now my motto is, "I can be spontaneous with twenty-four-hours' notice." Maybe that's why competing in this triathlon meant so much to us. Maybe we were trying to recapture some of our adventurous spirit—or prove that we still had it after all.

That morning, with my mind wandering to the past, I was surprised to find myself back to the turtle again. The turtle wasn't worried. The third time I passed by, I could tell that she had a goal to reach the shaded grass at the edge of the street. It was getting later and I considered moving her out of harm's way, but I didn't. I felt like that would cheat her out of the satisfaction of reaching her goal.

Kristin and I were turtles once. That was the time I talked her into running a marathon. We were young and healthy, we thought. How hard could it be? We stuffed thirteen Fig Newtons in our fanny packs, made matching T-shirts that read "Slow and steady finishes the race," and painted turtles on the front. "Go turtle girls," the spectators shouted as we plodded by. We found out that running twenty-six miles is harder than we thought ... but we did it!

It was my training for our triathlon that brought me to the turtle. Every time I rode by that turtle, I checked on her progress. She became symbolic for me. *If she can reach her goal*, I thought, *so can I!* Some Native Americans believe the turtle is a symbol of strength and perseverance; I've always liked that. When the turtle finally reached the edge, I felt privileged to witness her success. She continued into the grass and I lost sight of her.

As I rode down the hill, I thought of a punch line for my joke. "Why did the turtle cross the road? To live her life!" And that's what we are still doing every day—we turtle girls— slowly but surely.

ANXIETY GIRL TACKLES FLYING

My best friend, Kristin, is an Adventure Girl. We've been through a lot of adventures together. Our first adventures were in a Dilbert-like office where our job descriptions lacked a creative outlet, so we made up our own. We often plotted from our perch on the steps outside—with two spoons and a pint of Ben & Jerry's Cherry Garcia between us. An opportunity arose for us to embark on a real adventure together: teaching outdoor education in a remote part of Alabama while living in a log cabin on top of a mountain. Our new job description was hiking, rock climbing, facilitating a ropes course, teaching, singing, and playing. Weekends we traveled to the Smoky Mountains to camp in pouring rain, to Mardi Gras, to the St. Patrick's Day parade in Savannah.

We were passionate about our jobs and our lives. The passion translated to new opportunities. After our adventures, I returned to school to complete a graduate degree in education, and she studied for a master's in social work. Through it all, our adventures continued: a marathon, crazy weekend biking trips, triathlons.

Soon we included husbands and then babies in our adventures. But along the way of "growing up" and becoming responsible for our families, a little seed of anxiety sprouted and grew. Like kudzu, it spread, creeping around until it took over parts of our lives.

One manifestation of the anxiety was my fear of flying. After several years of avoiding airplanes, I decided to fly. It wasn't easy. In the weeks before my flight, I would burst into tears just thinking about it. Even seeing airplanes in the sky made my stomach tight. I spent more time focused on the ninety-minute flight than I did thinking about my destination. Here's what I learned:

Think about the destination. Whenever you start feeling anxious about flying, force yourself to picture a safe landing. Picture yourself walking off of the plane feeling happy. Anticipate the adventures of your vacation.

Plan distractions. I can't focus enough to read on a plane, but I like to work on easy crossword puzzles and look at the pictures in *People* magazines. Think of something you enjoy to occupy your mind.

Invest in good headphones. Airplanes are loud and have lots of weird noises. Bring along a playlist with lots of happy songs and some really good noise cancelling headphones.

Set small goals. Break up the trip into fifteen-minute segments. Decide on a reward each time. My rewards always involve chocolate.

Meditate. Sometimes I wonder what would happen if, instead of worrying about everything and praying as a last resort, I prayed about everything and worried as a last resort? I write down Bible verses, such as Philippians 4:6, on index cards and carry them with me on the flight. "Do not be anxious about anything, but in every situation, by prayer and petition, with thanksgiving, present your requests to God."

Medicate. Some people like a glass of wine to take the edge off. I got myself so worked up about my overseas flight that I finally talked to my doctor. She prescribed a small dose of Xanax, which really helped.

Write. I bring my journal on the plane and write through my anxiety in real time. Here's an excerpt of an entry from one of my flights:

> *8:35 a.m.: I feel nauseous, on the verge of tears, and a little shaky. I've already gone to the bathroom about six times this morning—my bladder succumbing to a constant state of "nervous pees."*

8:45 a.m.: My heart is pounding and I feel a bit of bile collecting at the base of my throat.

8:47 a.m.: We are moving!

9:30 a.m.: We're going through some clouds. The plane is swaying and bumping. I know the turbulence is normal, but I feel a surge of tightness in my chest again. Regretting the decision to get coffee. The friendly flight attendant filled my cup to the brim and it's too hot to drink. I am picturing the turbulence spilling it all over my lap.

9:40 a.m.: I dab my overactive armpits discreetly with my beverage napkin.

10:00 a.m.: I'm glad to have finished my coffee.

10:10 a.m.: We're starting our descent. Only twenty more minutes in the air. Homestretch—I can do it!

And last but not least …

Define yourself. If you think of yourself as Anxiety Girl, you will be anxious. You are Adventure Girl, able to fly high above the sky on the way to your newest adventure. You can do it!

TRIATHLON REPORT

On the day of my first triathlon, I set my alarm for 4:40 a.m., but the sound of the pouring rain woke me up instead. Not the ideal weather conditions I was hoping for. I plugged in the coffee pot, grabbed a PB&J and a banana, and pulled on my swimsuit and a pair of shorts.

We arrived at the site of the triathlon when it was still dark and raining. I wandered through the maze of racks until I found the one for my number, 329. I hooked up my bike and grabbed my sweatshirt, leaving everything else in the waterproof bag. Normally, people lay out everything they need for easy access, but I wanted to keep my stuff dry as long as possible.

"Body marking!" a volunteer called, holding a big fat Sharpie marker.

"Here!" I replied. He wrote 329 down the sides of my arms and on each thigh. Then he drew a 42 on the back of my calf to show my age.

Properly marked, I headed over to the line to pick up

my timing chip. It was encased in a waterproof shell that I secured to my ankle with Velcro.

Last stop, the bathroom. *If I ever do this again, I'm getting a two-piece*, I thought as I peeled off all my layers to pee.

By 6:45 a.m., five hundred women were gathered by the edge of the pool, ready for the first event. We stood as *The Star-Spangled Banner* played and the race began. Five hundred women cannot jump into the pool and start swimming laps all together, so we were seeded by our estimated swim time. The faster swimmers started first and then every fifteen seconds a new triathlete began. By estimating my swim at about twelve minutes, I was one of the slower swimmers and would be the 329th person in the pool. I had a while to wait.

While we were waiting and watching, I saw a woman I had met in the bathroom line. She had just learned how to swim and was really nervous about getting in the pool. "You've got this," I'd told her. "If you panic, just put your feet down. It is a pool." Now that she was in the water, she was panicking. There were too many swimmers—feet kicking, water splashing. She stood up, looking like she was going to cry. "You've got this," I yelled to her. She started to move forward—not swimming but jogging in the pool. Other spectators began to cheer, "You can do it!"

Slowly she made her way up and down the lanes. By the last lane, we were all cheering for her and she wore a wide and proud grin. That's the kind of triathlon this was—more supportive than competitive.

Finally, it was my turn. "Ready, go." I pushed off the wall and began to freestyle down my first lap. I swam up and down the first lane, then ducked under the lane line and swam up and back again. This is called a snake swim. I swam 8 laps for a total of 400 meters. Done! I pushed my body out of the pool and ran down to the transition area. Thankfully, the pouring rain had stopped, but a gentle mist was falling.

I tried not to worry too much as I dried off, pulled on my sneakers and shorts, and buckled my helmet. The bike was usually my easy leg, but I had never biked in the rain. I walked my bike to the mounting line and hopped on. I worried about my tire traction. I worried about skidding. I worried about visibility. Because I was being extra cautious, the first few miles were slower than normal. At some point, though, I forgot to worry and started to enjoy it all—the water dripping off my helmet onto my nose, my burning muscles as I pushed up the hills, the spectators waving and cheering. I rode eleven miles and returned to the transition area, racked my bike, and switched my biking helmet for a baseball cap.

Now it was time for the run. If you have never felt the sensation of riding a bike and then trying to run, try it sometime. Your legs feel like bricks. After having struggled with a recent hip injury for the last few months, I wasn't even sure if I would be able to run. I started jogging, slow and easy, trying to loosen up my legs. "Slow and easy," I kept telling myself. "Walk if you need to."

The rain was picking up again as I crossed the street to

run around the lake. Slowly, I made my way around. One mile, slow and easy. Two miles, slow and easy. *I'm doing it! I'm almost there!* The third mile ended with a long incline. I leaned into the hill and looked up to the top—there was my cheering section! They were decked out in pink, holding a poster and calling my name.

This was it! I pushed up the hill and around the field to the finish. I started to sprint, but the field was like a giant marsh from all the rain. I ran as fast as I could to cross the finish line. *I did it, despite the rain, despite the worry, despite my injury. I did it!*

LESSONS FROM THE HALF MARATHON

I've ridden my bike across the steamy cornfields of Iowa in July and run a marathon through Washington, DC, in the pouring rain. I've run a relay race through pitch black at 2 a.m. on the sandy peninsula of Cape Cod and blindly breaststroked through the choppy Atlantic Ocean during a triathlon. I love training for races for two reasons: they push me out of my comfort zone, and I always learn something along the way. Here are a few lessons from a recent half marathon:

1. Don't eat taco chicken before your long run. Just don't.

2. Peer pressure can be a good thing—because I never, ever, in a million years ever thought I would run 13.1 miles again ... until some friends talked me into the "opportunity."

3. Razors are a runner's friend. Armpit stubble and long runs don't go together.

4. Run with an amazing person, such as my friend Debbie. The right running partner will motivate you, inspire you, and make the time fly by with witty stories. Don't run with Debbie, though, because then she might be too tired to run with me. Selfishly, I don't want to share her, so go find your own running partner.

5. When sending encouraging text messages to other runners, always proofread. Otherwise, your phone might autocorrect "I'm giving you a big hoorah!" to "I'm giving you a big wet rash." Then no one will want to room with you in the hotel.

6. When training for a half marathon, try to avoid the never-ending winter of the Polar Vortex, if at all possible. It snowed on my first day of training in December. It snowed, rained, sleeted, froze—you name it—literally every week of training all the way through March including the day of the race.

7. Ignore the myth that running helps you lose weight. If you are unable to avoid the Polar Vortex, you'll need some extra layers anyway. Use this as an excuse to carb-load like crazy. Start early, eat often. But, as previously mentioned, just not taco chicken.

8. Make the race far enough away that you need a

hotel room. People keep asking, "How was the race?" Hmmm, I ran for two and a half hours. It was freezing cold and windy. Torrential downpours brought flood warnings. And my phone was sitting in a bag of rice trying to dry out from the whole ordeal. But it was still fabulous! I didn't cook, clean, grocery shop, pay bills, mediate teenage bickering, run errands, or grade papers. I was with good friends. We talked. We laughed. We dined in real restaurants. Which brings me to my last lesson …

9. Set a goal—13.1 miles in Philadelphia, check. What's next, friends? Moab in October or New Orleans in November? Key West in January or Nashville in April?

I'm ready to train for our next adventure. I've already started carb-loading!

IN IRELAND, YOU CAN ALWAYS FIND A BED

As much as I try to think through every last detail, I never know what will happen when I travel. Travel is the perfect antidote to my perfectionist tendencies because I have to expect the unexpected—some unexpected moments turn out to be highlights of the trip, while others make great stories only after we've survived.

My own epiphany about travel came during a sermon about Epiphany when our pastor contrasted the stories of the shepherds and the wise men. In the story, the angel gives the shepherds specific directions about where to go, who they will find there, and what to expect. In contrast, the magi see a light and decide to follow it. They aren't sure where they are going or where their journey will take them, but they have faith in their decision.

Admittedly, I often wish my Christian journey were like that of the shepherds. If only I could hear God's voice loud and clear telling me what lies ahead. Instead, I am learning how to be like the magi. I'm learning to make decisions based on faith even though I'm not sure where I'm headed. For me, traveling is always a leap of faith. Here is a summary of a few of my leaps.

Arkansas: the road less traveled

Debbie and I jumped in the car to head northwest to the Ozarks. We were in search of a scenic hike near the Buffalo River called Whitaker Point. Heading west on the highway, we eventually turned up a winding road. The Ozarks are not a very populated part of Arkansas, as we discovered. We had planned to stop for gas at one of the many towns dotting the map along our route. However, all we could see as we passed through these towns was the occasional old home or post office. Just when I was beginning to really worry, we hit Ponca. Population 13 must be the magic number because we found a gas station and a store! From there, we turned on a small dirt and gravel road and slowly made our way to the trailhead. Where were we? No signal on my phone and no trailhead in sight, but we persevered. Our efforts were rewarded with a beautiful four-mile hike and views of the valley.

Chicago: the plane less traveled

We only made it halfway home from Arkansas. We flew into Chicago and learned that our connecting flight had been canceled. Apparently, all the flights to our area were canceled due to some kind of flypocalypse. Deciding to make the best

of an unplanned evening in Chicago, we checked into our
hastily booked hotel and took the L downtown, arriving at
5:00 p.m. So many things to do, so little time! We started
with a walk around Millennium Park, caught an architectural
boat tour, found some Chicago deep dish pizza at Giordano's,
and rode the elevator to the top of the John Hancock Center.
Not bad for one night!

Florida: the path less traveled
The "Ding" Darling National Wildlife Refuge was a short
drive from our resort. We spent the morning at the visitor
center learning about the wildlife there. The park rangers
really knew how to appeal to the kids. "Wanna hear about
farting manatees?" one asked. "Cool, huh?" We were excited
to take the loop hike through the mangrove forest to make
some animal sightings of our own. Until we realized the wide
gravel path provided no shade at all. Hiking 4 miles in the
90 degree midday sun was rather uncomfortable and quiet.
Too quiet. There was not an animal in sight. They were all
hiding in the shade questioning the common sense of humans,
I suppose. Finally, we saw an alligator cooling in the mud,
but not before Jack had declared this the worst day of his
tortured, sweaty life.

Ireland: the bed less slept in
We were traveling to the Dingle Peninsula for the day. Since
it was a two-and-a-half-hour drive from our apartment in

Bunratty, we decided to spend the night at a B&B. The arrangements were made and confirmed with a lovely woman named Veronica Houlihan. We took our time getting there, stopping along the peninsula to enjoy the views and play on the beach. When we finally arrived late afternoon, no one answered our knock on the door. We tried to contact her with no success. Finally, we decided to ask the shopkeeper next door if he knew her. "Oh, yes, I know Veronica Houlihan. A shame about her husband's brother, isn't it now? And the funeral's today."

Have any idea how long an Irish funeral lasts? Neither did we. We wandered around town a bit. Still not home. We ate dinner in a pub. Still not home. We ate ice cream at Murphy's. Still not home. We played cards. Finally, we decided we needed to try Plan B. We started driving along the road looking for B&Bs with vacancy signs. When we found one, I would run up to see if they could accommodate the four of us. Three more times we struck out. Paul was starting to think about having to drive back to Bunratty.

"Give me one more chance," I pleaded. We stopped again. A woman answered the door. I told her my story. "Come in," she said. "In Ireland, you can always find a bed." We had a great night's sleep and a full Irish breakfast in the morning.

It's true: in Ireland, you can always find a bed.

PUPPIES ARE LIKE THAT

Having a puppy is not like flying on an airplane. Before takeoff, airline attendants always take time to explain the emergency procedures. "Should the cabin lose pressure, oxygen masks will drop from the overhead area. Please place the mask over your own mouth and nose before assisting others." In other words, take care of yourself first—then help others.

Puppies aren't like that. When they wake up at 5:00 a.m., you can't have a rational conversation with them. You can't say, "It's too early—go back to bed." They don't understand the phrase, "Give me five minutes to brew a pot of coffee and then I'll play with you." Puppies come first. Because if you ignore them, they will pee on the kitchen floor and chew on the chair leg. Puppies are like that.

When our kids were little, we read them a board book called *Puppies Are Like That.* Having a puppy is a surefire cure to perfectionism.

When our old dog, Tatum, passed away and the kids left

for college, our house felt a little empty. Was it time to add a new furry companion to the family? We decided (okay, I decided, but Paul is the best husband ever) to foster a puppy and reacquaint ourselves with the joy and commitment of having a pet.

Here's what I knew about fostering before agreeing to care for a puppy:

- All the puppies are cute.
- Wolf Trap Animal Rescue provides all the supplies you need.
- If you fall in love, you have priority to adopt the puppy (this is known as "foster failing").

What more did I need to know? Sign me up!

Here's what I learned about fostering after agreeing to care for a puppy named Claudette:

- Puppies may have heartworm, fleas, parvovirus, or even mange.
- The change in diet may mean nausea and diarrhea.
- The puppy will need to be spayed or neutered.
- The puppy should not be left alone for more than four or five hours at a time.

I don't tell you this to scare you but to remind you of the reality that there's a lot more to puppies than cuteness.

Because pictures of puppies on Instagram tug at our heartstrings. And you cannot raise a puppy on warm fuzzies alone. It takes blood, sweat, and tears. Literally. Furthermore, this is an important time in the life of the puppy. The socialization period occurs in puppies at approximately three to twelve weeks. We cared for Claudette when she was most impressionable. It was a huge responsibility and one we took seriously. And, by the way, she is the cutest. Puppy. Ever.

Here's a summary of our lives during our three weeks of fostering:

- Arrange our schedules to tag-team puppy time in four-hour increments.
- Talk about poop a lot. "Did she poop?" "What time did she last poop?"
- Hire a dog sitter to come over on occasions when we need to be gone longer.
- Bundle up in the cold darkness for early morning/ late night potty breaks.
- Clean up accidents in the house.
- Purchase extra toys to play with the puppy.
- Make sure the puppy is getting plenty of exercise.
- Work on training the puppy.
- Arrange for "meet and greets" with potential adopters.
- Read a book on how to raise a puppy.
- Distract the puppy from chewing.

And oh, the puppy chewing. That's where the blood, sweat, and tears come in. Those puppy teeth are razor sharp! I remembered very quickly to put the electric cords up and keep my shoes in the closet. Anything on or near the floor was fair game. Including the carpet in my living room. Oops. Puppies are like that.

Puppy snuggles made up for all the hard work. Even in the short time we had her, Claudette's sweet personality emerged. She was a smart puppy who came to us already crate trained and sleeping through the night. She knew "come" and "go potty" and loved to chew sticks and chase balls. She loved to be scratched behind her ears and to snuggle up next to you when she was tired. When you said her name, she gave you a little head tilt as if to respond, "Yes? I'm listening?"

Everyone thought we would "foster fail." We didn't. The house feels quiet again. Empty. We may foster again and someday, perhaps, we will get another dog. But for right now I'm excited to have a conversation with Paul that doesn't revolve around poop.

YOGA

This is the story about how I (who am not a yoga person AT ALL) have a new hobby and it is, of all things, yoga. I still don't think of myself as a "yogi." I'm not a touchy-feely person. I'm not a hugger. So, the thought of being in a room with a bunch of people chanting "Om" doesn't appeal to me. And what's the deal with the third eye on the forehead? My son already thinks I have eyes in the back of my head, and that's quite enough extra eyes for me. Also, for some reason, I think of yoga and vegetarians as going hand in hand. I know, I'm generalizing. Some of my best friends are vegetarians. Still, I can't imagine giving up bacon and, somehow, I think that means I am not a candidate for yoga.

Another reason I never tried yoga before: I thought it was all about stretching. I know stretching is good for you, just like flossing is good for you alongside a whole host of other things that I should do to improve my health. I've even read articles about red wine, coffee, and chocolate being good for you, which is just awesome. Really, I'm waiting for an article that says bacon is good for you, but I haven't come across it yet. If you see one, let me know. Anyway, for some reason, I have an easier time drinking wine and eating chocolate on a regular basis than I do flossing and stretching.

There I was, living peacefully in my yoga-free existence when along came my friend Debbie. She kept talking about yoga and how it made her happy. Debbie invited me as a guest to her class and, in a lapse of judgment, I agreed to go. Debbie and I have been friends for a long time, and I've known her to eat a piece of bacon or two. I figured I'd keep quiet about that so the people in the yoga studio wouldn't ostracize her.

I learned that there are many types of yoga and we were going to do Baptiste Power Vinyasa yoga. When the class began, I discovered that I am really bad at yoga. Well, that's not entirely true. I am pretty good at Child's Pose at the beginning, and Shavasana at the end. It is everything in between that needs work.

The class seemed to follow a certain rhythm. First, we did a bunch of poses that have funny names like Chaturanga Dandasana, but I wasn't fooled. Call a push-up by any other name—it is still a push-up. I was breaking a sweat, my heart rate was up, and I was fully aware of my pathetic lack of upper arm strength. Next came the balance poses, and I realized that I don't favor one side or the other—I am equally unco-ordinated on both sides. After wobbling about trying to stand on one foot for a while, I was relieved when we moved into the exercises for core strength ... only to discover abdominal muscles I didn't even know I had. Finally, we moved to stretching, and I conceded that my lack of regular commitment on this front had not helped my flexibility in any way.

Each time the instructor called out a new pose, I glanced around to see what everyone was doing before attempting it. But as horrible as I was, I actually liked it. Everyone was so focused on their own progress that no one was looking at my feeble, unskilled attempts. The class was fast paced, and I felt like I was getting a great workout. But the best part was the teacher. Along with his instruction, he gave us a pep talk, cheering us on as we went, pushing us to try a little harder and go a little further. It was like I'd signed up for a yoga class and they'd thrown in a ninety-minute motivational seminar for free. I decided to take advantage of a deal for new students and purchase a discounted class pack. *What the heck*, I thought, *I'll try another class or two.*

My family took notice of my second trip to the yoga studio. Be it coincidence, fate, or just plain luck, this was shortly before the holidays. My Christmas gifts that year included a yoga bag, yoga towel, yoga shirt, and book about yoga. I looked like a walking advertisement for Lululemon. I felt a bit like an imposter, especially when I couldn't hold Tree Pose for more than three seconds and there was too much sweat in my third eye for me to see anything clearly. I still don't like hugs and I still love bacon, but I'm beginning to rethink my opinion of yoga. I think I kind of like it.

Part VII

Summer Vacation

I have heard it said that winter, too, will pass,
that spring is a sign that summer is due at
last. See, all we have to do is hang on.

—Maya Angelou

BUYER BEWARE

Crying is funny to me because I'm a planner and I never plan to cry. But in certain situations when I'm not in control—of my emotions, my plans, or my health—the tears come.

Once, after a massage, I cried from the stress of the experience. Normally, there isn't room in my teaching salary budget for the luxury of a spa. So, I was pleasantly surprised and even a little excited on the last day of school to receive a gift card for a spa experience. I logged onto their website and clicked on the button to find a convenient location.

To kick off summer, I went in and had a lovely, relaxing massage. Relaxing, that is, until it was time to pay.

"Oh, we don't accept those gift cards," the woman at the front desk explained.

I tried to explain right back to her: they did indeed—I even looked it up on my phone and showed her the proof, but to no avail.

Handing over my Visa, I started to cry, right there in the middle of the spa. I was so embarrassed! So, I ended up paying for my own massage, what was the big deal? Why were my eyes turning into broken faucets?

Besides the fact that teachers don't make a boatload of money for discretionary spending, we also live in the land of teacher lingo. We don't "meet with coworkers," we "collaborate with our team." We dialogue and discuss. We practice the seven P's of collaboration: **P**ause, **P**araphrase, **P**robe, **P**ut ideas on the table, **P**resume **P**ositive Intentions … sometimes I feel so much like a **P**sychologist it makes me want to **P**uke.

So when I leave my bubble of the education world and step outside into the summer sunlight, I may be a little naïve to think the rest of the world operates the way I do. I am trustworthy, so I trust people. I am honest, so I believe others. As a consumer, I believe the salesperson wants to help me be a satisfied customer.

Not to sound overly dramatic (well, since you already saw me sniffling in the spa reception area, let's continue), but I think I started crying because I felt taken advantage of. I trusted the website and the person on the phone. I think I started crying because I "**p**resumed **p**ositive intentions" and someone didn't presume the same of me. I didn't want to be the cynical, distrustful consumer. It isn't in my nature.

That same week I was again made to feel like an unprepared consumer. Jack's big present for his sixteenth birthday was a pool table—in stock and ready for delivery! I called to figure out when it was coming since I hadn't heard from the store and they'd told me "end of July." How could an in-stock pool table take a month to get to my house? The store manager checked and returned my call.

"It's the legs," he told me. "The table is in stock, but the legs are coming from the warehouse." Okay, not to sound naïve again, but why would you have a pool table in stock without legs? Is there a big market for legless pool tables? I suggested possibly they could mail the legs instead of waiting for the truck delivery. Heck, where was the warehouse? Could I go pick up the legs? Clearly, the store manager had never lived with a teenager. He seemed in no hurry to think outside the box and help figure out a creative solution. Where I saw a woman "thinking outside the box," he saw a "crazy lady."

Again, I wanted to assume the store manager cared about me and wanted me to be a satisfied customer. But I was feeling a little jaded. Because it seemed the month-long delay in delivery was no longer his concern as long as he had his money.

When reviewing our annual school survey, I find it frustrating that parents are allowed to leave anonymous comments that are sometimes downright mean and hurtful. We are told we need to give parents an opportunity to express their level of satisfaction. "We're in the business of customer service," my assistant principal said. Yet, my experiences "in the real world" make me wonder what customer service means anymore.

Just when I'd decided to adopt the new motto "Buyer Beware" and become a distrustful, cynical person, the phone rang. It was the woman from the spa. She was calling to tell me she was sorry and shared her plan to fix the situation.

So, what did I do? I burst into tears again. This time because her kindness and concern restored my faith in humanity. It also made me wonder if I should go back to the pool table store and start to cry.

If being an honest, authentic person didn't get me what I wanted, maybe I'd have more luck as a blubbering crybaby.

CHANGE OF PLANS

The events I am about to describe are 100% true. I tell you this upfront lest you think I might exaggerate by embellishing some of the nonessential details for the sake of good storytelling.

This is the kind of story that is no fun at all when you are immersed in its unfolding. It is only weeks (Months? Years?) later when you can look back and laugh, ruefully, as you say, "Remember the weekend when ..."

But let me go back to the beginning. When coordinating summer plans and camps, I realized that, although on different schedules and in different states, the kids' summer camps overlapped on two glorious days. Let me repeat for emphasis: both children were scheduled to be out of town for the whole weekend!

Now, what were the odds that our youth pastor would be unable to fulfill his chaperone duties? When he called Paul with a request, "The baby isn't due for a few weeks, but I need a backup chaperone just in case," Paul was happy to be on call. What were the odds?

Superstitious people will say I jinxed the whole thing by telling people out loud how much I was looking forward to a weekend with Paul. When the call came Friday (no surprise—you saw that one coming) and he left to chaperone Katherine's camp, I was initially disappointed. Then I began to regroup and ponder the unimaginable. A weekend alone. The house all to myself! Whatever I chose to do would be uninterrupted! I could sit in front of the TV with a pint of Ben & Jerry's and not have to share a single spoonful.

Friday night I helped Jack pack. With his bulging duffel bag finally zipped and waiting by the door, I tucked him in and turned off the light. I closed my eyes, snuggled into my sheets, and started to drift off only to be interrupted.

"Mom? I don't feel good."

That's when the vomiting began. We scrambled to the bathroom. With each subsequent trip to the toilet, I felt more helpless. Other than offering a cool washcloth and murmuring my sympathies, there wasn't much I could do. For eight straight hours, the stomach virus wreaked havoc on Jack's system. I don't think I'd pulled an all-nighter since college, but neither of us slept. Sometime in the early morning hours, I realized going to camp was not an option. The bus was about to depart for Georgia and, rather than waving his goodbyes from the window, Jack was curled up in the fetal position on a towel on the bathroom floor.

Jack finally fell asleep mid-morning, at which point I

donned my yellow rubber gloves to disinfect the bathroom, start the first of several vomit-saturated loads of laundry, and consider the situation. Poor Jack. He had been looking forward to camp. Change of plans. Instead he would spend the weekend at home with his mother. I hoped when he woke up, we could try to salvage what was left of it.

I still had a movie and some ice cream. The new plan—two spoons.

DO-OVER

"This day is a do-over," my friend said to me one day as we stood outside the pool gate in our swimsuits. We thought it would be a brilliant idea to meet at the pool to visit and share adventures of our busy summers while the kids played and swam—only to realize that the pool was closed for swimming due to a dive meet.

Some days nothing seems to work out as planned. Do you ever have those days?

That morning I had somehow missed my dog-walking friends. I thought I was behind and ran to catch up, but I was actually ahead. In the afternoon, a simple task of reserving airline tickets to Boston turned into a ninety-minute headache of a phone call. (Don't get me started on award miles reservations.) And the day ended at the closed pool gate.

Of course, we've all had days like that. Really, though, my question should be, "Did you ever have a day where everything went exactly as planned?" Because that is the holy grail of organization. Maybe it's just a myth, yet somehow I come to believe in it every morning. I have lists and schedules. I have a budget. I have my house divided into quadrants and my life organized in a daily planner and time map. Every day I wake up with the expectation that it will all go according to plan. And, somehow, every day I am surprised when it doesn't.

"Life is difficult."[7] This is the first sentence in the book *The Road Less Traveled* by M. Scott Peck. Years ago, my friend Kristin and I tried to read this book together. "Life is a series of problems," Peck writes. "Do we want to moan about them or solve them?"[8] I can't tell you much more—despite our intentions, Kristin and I never made it past the first chapter. "Best book we never read," she told me. We still refer to that first sentence, though, when we're commiserating about a particularly lousy day.

Besides accepting that life has challenges, I can also reflect on things with a new perspective.

That morning I ran three miles—exercising the dog and me at the same time. What an unexpected bonus!

I accrued enough frequent flier miles to secure four airline tickets to Boston with no out-of-pocket expenses. How lucky!

And as the kids wandered off to play and watch the dive meet, I was sitting in the shade on a grassy hill catching up with a good friend.

---

7 M. Scott Peck, *The Road Less Traveled* (New York: Touchstone, 2003), 15.

8 M. Scott Peck, *The Road Less Traveled.*

It wasn't a "do-over" day. It wasn't even a "do-differently" day. I've got tomorrow for that.

A BOX OF MEMORIES

I still have the best present I've ever received. The box wasn't wrapped; in fact, it was empty when my grandfather gave it to me. Over the years, this box has become special for many reasons, including the memories I have of its beginnings.

As a kid, the highlight of every summer was driving up to Pennsylvania to spend a week with my grandparents. My grandpa spent most of his day in his "shop." The shop was a converted garage that housed his workbench and tools. It always smelled distinctly like his pipes, his wood-burning stove, and the sweet aroma of sawdust. It was in Grandpa's shop that I learned to putter. I learned to hammer nails, to smooth a board with sandpaper, and to trap a two-by-four in a vice grip. The object of being in the shop was not to build something specific; it was just to enjoy each other's company.

Our project inspirations came from looking in the scrap pile. Sometimes, our creations were simple—a car made from an old orange juice can. Sometimes, they were more elaborate—a set of Barbie furniture, complete with carefully fashioned wire hangers for Barbie's dresses. Sometimes, we weren't quite sure what we'd created. "Well, look at that crazy contraption," Grandpa would say affectionately as we looked at the abstract collage of nails and boards.

"Whaddya think, Nosilla, is it JUNK?" It probably was junk in someone else's eyes, but to Grandpa and me, each of our endeavors was a masterpiece.

During the summer of third grade, I came to Grandpa's shop with a special request. I wanted a box with a lock. Some of my Halloween candy had mysteriously disappeared, and I was suspicious of my little brother. I felt sure a lock box would keep Bobby's sticky hands away from my Reese's Peanut Butter Cups.

Grandpa helped me find good scraps for my box. He rummaged around to dig up hinges. We carefully measured and cut the pieces, and he helped me hammer them together without hitting my fingers. When we were finished, he painted it bright red with an A on top. Then he presented me with a real lock and key.

My lock box did successfully protect many years' worth of Halloween stashes. (My mother eventually confessed that it was she, not Bobby, who had a weakness for peanut butter cups.) As I grew older, the box became the hiding place for secret diaries and lists of boys who were cute. In high school, and later in college, it evolved into a keepsake box filled with athletic letters, concert ticket stubs, dried corsages, and pictures.

Today, the box is a symbol of the values Grandpa instilled in me. The time I spent working in Grandpa's shop helped build in me a sense of confidence, a sense of pride in accomplishing things myself, and a sense of honor to do a job right. Grandpa's patience in teaching a seven-year-old girl to hammer, saw, and paint paid off. When I moved into my first house, I wallpapered my own kitchen, hung my own curtains, and painted my own bedroom.

It's been over forty years since Grandpa made my lock box. The red paint is worn away in places, and the hinges are orange with rust, but I still have the original lock and key. As mementos in the box have changed over the years, so has my appreciation of the box itself. I realize that it is also a symbol of one of my favorite memories—my summers puttering with my grandfather, when he showed me, in so many ways, how much he loved me.

ONE NAP SHORT OF PERFECT

Some days I wake up and think, *Today is supposed to be perfect.* Perfect cloudless sky. Perfect temperature. Today will be the first perfect day.

Except …

Except I just need to do a few things before I begin my perfect day. Like fold six loads of laundry. Like buy milk. Like walk the dog. I should probably straighten up a bit.

So what if the morning is spent on chores and errands? The afternoon will be perfect.

Except …

Except that I can't seem to decide what to do. Should I sit on the patio and read? Head to the pool and take a swim? Ride my bike? Suddenly I feel very tired. I will just put my head down for a minute. Then I will decide.

Except a minute turns into an afternoon nap. I wake up feeling groggy. I look at the clock. Today was supposed to be a perfect day. And I slept through it.

I recognize that my body was exhausted. There will be

other days for the pool, the patio, and the pedaling. Today I was just too tired to be perfect. Every time I have another imperfect day, I learn something. I learn how to deal with disappointment and adapt to change, how to look for silver linings and find ways to help others. My imperfections have pushed me out of my comfort zone, and I have pushed back with creativity, innovation, and resilience. Striving for perfection has taught me how much I don't yet know and how much I have to learn. It has reminded me of my strengths and humbled me with my shortcomings.

I dreamt of someday writing a book called *Confessions of a Reformed Perfectionist*. Problem was, I thought I'd actually have to reform. And here's my confession: I'm not reformed. I'm still a perfectionist at heart, but I'm learning how to recognize when it is an asset and when it's getting in the way of my happiness and my relationships.

I still wake up every morning determined to be the best me I can be. I still wake up every morning and remind myself that I am not in control. All I can do is control the way I respond to whatever arises—with a grin, some grit, and a bit of grace.

ACKNOWLEDGMENTS

I wanted to write a book with fifty chapters to celebrate my fiftieth birthday. This was a crazy idea for a few reasons:

- I didn't know how to write a book. Most of my knowledge about writing a book is based on a fictional character in the telenovela *Jane the Virgin*.
- My spelling isn't the greatest. I once came in third place in a spelling bee, but there were only three contestants. Sometimes I'm not smarter than a fifth grader.
- I don't know all the grammar rules. I usually go by intuition, and I can't always explain why I think a comma goes where I've put it. I'm not sure what a dangling participle is, but I keep meaning to look it up.
- I'm not sure who will read my book besides my mom.

Still, it's good to have goals. I'm a teacher—I'm used to being creative and resourceful. And I know when to ask for help. This book never would have been a reality without the help and support of my favorite editors and my family. Thank you, Camille, Stu, Kristin, Paul, and Mom for reading my earliest drafts and offering feedback and suggestions. Thank you, Paige, Kristie, and the rest of the Archangel Ink team for your editing and design expertise.

Writing a book was not easy. But, thankfully, I'm a whiz with the binding machine in the teacher workroom, so publishing will be a piece of cake.

IMAGINARY BACK COVER BLURBS

When I was dreaming up imaginary back cover blurbs, here's who I thought of asking and what I imagined they might say:

Allison is a whiz with the binding machine, and we have the same birthday, so she's all right with me. This book is a bit of whimsy you'll definitely want to pick up when you visit my Nowhere Bookshop.

—Jenny Lawson (The Bloggess)[9]

If you ever think you are not cut out to be a writer, that is just your doubts and fears talking. You have to keep writing. You are a writer.

—Jane Villanueva, *Jane the Virgin*[10]

---

9 You'll remember that I read Jenny's blog about a metal chicken named Beyoncé.

10 Fictional characters probably don't write back cover blurbs, but when I'm chatting with Jane the Virgin, this is what I imagine she says.

Allison's writing is much better than her banjo playing.

—Scott Avett, The Avett Brothers[11]

Allison is so insightful and clever. She is the best daughter, and her writing is wonderful.

—Sissa, the author's mother[12]

What I know for sure—you should read this book! You get a copy, and you get a copy!

—Oprah, no introduction needed[13]

---

11 Scott Avett is my favorite banjo player! I hope he'll love my book so much that I'll score backstage passes to my next The Avett Brothers concert.

12 My mom already compliments my writing, so she'll be a natural.

13 If I'm going to dream big on these back cover blurbs, why not?

ABOUT THE AUTHOR

Allison B. Kelly is the author of the memoir-in-essays *There's Spaghetti on my Ceiling: And Other Confessions of a Reformed Perfectionist.* She is an elementary school teacher with a master's degree in education and endorsements in gifted education and ESL. She's an early riser and list maker who survived raising two teenagers while keeping sane by running, biking, and traveling. Allison lives in Virginia with her family.